You're Richer Than You Think!

A Step by Step Guide to building a lasting

financial legacy for your family.

Sabine K. Franco, Esq

To: Cameron
Happy Legacy Building

Dedication

To my husband Steven and daughter Lauren, Thank you for inspiring me to be great. Thank you for motivating me to leave a meaningful legacy.

Table of Contents

Introduction

L egacy Planning compliments the estate planning process. Its primary focus is on intangible assets. One of the most crucial aspects of creating an inheritance is its capability to sustain an enduring presence that extends beyond the duration of one's life. Although physical assets are considered as part of an individual's legacy, the importance of the history of institutions or families, as well as values and the stories that define us, suggests that each family, individual, and organization can benefit by implementing an effective plan for a legacy.

I'm often asked, "How much money do I need to have in order to plan for my legacy?" Potential clients are very motivated and interested in planning, but some are unsure if their finances are sufficient to undertake something like that.

My response is simple, "You don't need a lot of money to start but you do need to start if you plan on leaving a meaningful legacy." There is a misconception that you have to be rich before you begin planning. That couldn't be further from the truth.

Every day all across the world, people wake up thinking they have more time to plan and take care of their future. Often, they say, "Tomorrow I'll start my investment plan, tomorrow I will live well," or "Tomorrow, I will find my purpose and do all the things I aspire to do." In essence, they are saying, "I'll wait to build my legacy. I just need to focus on what's going on now." They miss the big picture. Unfortunately, for many, that same mindset has caused families all sorts of financial pain, heartbreak, and frustration because of unforeseen accidents, untimely sickness, or leaving the family upside down after a loved one passes away without the right protection. Avoiding situations like this is the whole purpose of having a plan for asset protection and a good foundation for asset creation.

The truth is, life happens, mistakes happen. One thing is for certain, you will never make it out of life alive, and that is exactly why asset protection should be taken seriously. Many successful, famous, wealthy people have died without protecting their assets, indirectly hanging their families out to dry by giving away all or most of their wealth and everything they worked hard for to the government. This is why it is imperative we know what our goals and dreams are. We must plan well and take some action every day of our lives to manifest that plan. This is how we create a lasting legacy that we are proud of.

When you think about legacy, what does it really mean to you? What does it mean to create a name for yourself, so big that the world knows you by your last name and in doing so creates opportunities and access for generations to follow? You may be thinking; how can you create that legacy with not much to start with because you didn't come from a wealthy family or you're barely surviving.

The truth is, whatever your current condition may be, many successful people started in the same position as you. You're richer than you think!

Creating your legacy for your family is not only about having a dream and going for it, there are several other major steps involved in creating wealth and making an impact. The financial part of legacy creation is extremely crucial. It's important that you are covered when you are on the journey of pursuing your purpose.

When I say "You're richer than you think," I'm saying that no matter where you are in life, you can start right now with a few simple strategies to build a lasting legacy for your family.

CHAPTER 1

Creating a Legacy

"Discipline is doing the things today to protect your future that others are not willing to do so you can leave a legacy that others only dream of."

— Sabine K. Franco

Every day I wake up, I am constantly thinking of the legacy I'm creating. The benefits I can leave to the world to have traveled this path. I think about my husband, my daughter, my business, and how the world would be different because I was here. While it's great to think about it, I know it's much more important to create a plan to ensure the family I love, as well as generations to follow, will be protected.

Throughout my career I have had the pleasure of meeting many great people from all walks of life. As an asset protection attorney, I have an incredible opportunity to help families ensure they are properly set up for their futures. One of the things I am often troubled to hear is how little value people place on their lives, particularly their future. By value, I mean how causally they prepare or fail to prepare for the future. They instead focus on current adversities, past challenges and circumstances instead of focusing on and doing the small things today that would lead to creating a better tomorrow.

In speaking with a client recently, he expressed that he was so motivated to plan his legacy because he didn't want to end up like his dad. His dad, in his 70's, had no retirement plan, no pension, and nothing to show for the life he lived, or that reflected his motivation to live a life of meaning. The lack of value, unfortunately, stems from the preceding generations. The lack of information, the teachings, disciplines, and fear is something that continues to be passed on through generations. What doesn't change for any of us, is that one day, as hard as it may be to grasp, we don't have forever on this earth, so the question always is:

> *"What do you want to leave behind when you are gone?"*

Let's be honest, with the hustle and bustle of today, we have jobs, businesses, school, marriage, children, bills, vacations, and so many things happening at such a fast pace. When do we have time to sit down and plan for the very things we are working for or to keep? When it comes down to it, leaving a meaningful legacy means simply knowing that if you died today, you would be happy with being known for whatever you created while living. Everyone will leave a legacy whether they like it or not. This can't be opted out of. You want to be sure the legacy you leave is something that your future will thank you for. For a moment, think about what your legacy will say about you right now, and then ask yourself is it something you are proud of? If the answer is no, and you have been putting off establishing a proper legacy, then I will be showing you simple strategies throughout this book that can effectively ensure your legacy lives on long after you are gone in the most memorable way. You don't need to be famous or have a lot of money to protect your future, and if you haven't up to this point, I want to encourage you to do so.

The types of legacies many of us unfortunately find ourselves in are due to:

- ⊙ Family before us not understanding the importance of planning
- ⊙ Being misinformed that verbally expressed desires is enough
- ⊙ Believing there is plenty of time to get started.
- ⊙ Believing a certain amount of money is needed before getting started

While it's very motivating to talk about the lives we will impact, or the value we will impart on our kids, it's equally as important that we think about what tangible assets we will leave behind for our survivors. Nothing is more embarrassing than to work so hard all of your life and like my client's dad, have absolutely nothing to show for it simply because you didn't have a big picture to aim for. It is okay if you aren't swimming in money, you don't have to be. The average person is not, but what you will find is *You're Richer Than You Think,* when you realize you have more value than you think with what you currently have.

The Power of Legacy Creating

When you think of the word "legacy" what is the first thought that comes to your mind? What does the word legacy mean to you? What do you want it to be? What is that one thing that you want to spend your entire life doing and to be remembered by when you are gone?

To some, it might be a cause or mission–how the world would be a different place because they created something. To others it may mean starting a business which in turn creates wealth or streams of income for their family and generations to follow. Legacy has different meanings to different people, and all of those things that legacy might mean to them are perfectly accurate as there cannot be any right or wrong definitions for the individual. When you look up the definition of legacy it simply means what is passed from one generation to the next, and typically in the form of property, gifts, or money. However, as long as you define what legacy means for you and it motivates, challenges, inspires, and drives you to leave a mark on the world because you were here and you lived and lived well, that's all that matters.

Here is one thing to think about: "Your legacy doesn't need to be one big thing, it may be a series of small, impactful things you have built to change the lives of others.

Legacy is anything that:

- ⊙ Reflects your personality and values
- ⊙ Inspires others in a positive way
- ⊙ Represents the way you'll be remembered when you've gone

Building a lasting legacy for your family and the lives of others is not something to just take lightly. A good man or woman leaves an inheritance to their children and children's children. It's something you are responsible for and should be your entire life's mission. Not something you continue to put off because the conversation seems uneasy, or you are waiting until all of your ducks are lined up in a row. That's not the best approach to take. It's also important to understand that it's not something that you can magically do at the last minute when time is running out. When we place a high value on ourselves and our purpose here on earth, looking at the bigger picture is all that will matter. It's as simple as that.

Your Legacy Mission Statement

When George Bernard Shaw, the Nobel Prize winning Irish Playwright was on his deathbed, he was asked if he could live his life over again, what would he do differently? His response was, "I'd be the person I could have been, but never was." Every day we have people on the news making history, fulfilling their goals, and living up to their legacy. But what do you think about yourself? The time for living is limited. If you've never considered that question before, you're not alone. Many people are so immersed in their daily activities that they do not think about the way their actions can affect the legacy they leave for their spouses, friends, parents, children, and the rest of the world to observe.

"Yeah," you say, "but does my legacy really matter?"

Of course, it does. It's as simple as not repeating the same steps that prior generations have, but instead doing something different with what you've learned and how you've been impacted by it. The waves that you create have the ability to alter the flow of life in the direction of those you cherish. In the film *Gladiator*, the character Maximus declared, "What we do in life echoes through eternity."

Know Your Mission.

First, a legacy worthy of remembrance and pride must have a primary goal in your life. Many have had the pleasure of hearing about mission statements for businesses, however, creating a mission statement for your personal life is quite different. Imagine it as a powerful inspirational message that will guide all aspects of your life.

Ideally, the personal mission statement should consist of a concise, easily remembered sentence or bullet points or a paragraph that outlines your dreams and goals. It serves one purpose: to help you when making crucial decisions that impact how you live your life. While you can choose not to let anyone in on the details of your mission, you should live your life in such a way that others near you should be able to discern the purpose of your mission in light of your words, attitudes, and actions.

When creating your mission statement, **you should consider the following aspects:**

- ⊙ Your goal(s).
- ⊙ What purpose inspires you?
- ⊙ What higher callings do you believe you were created to fulfill on this planet?
- ⊙ What are the core values you never compromise on?
- ⊙ What principles would you die to defend?
- ⊙ What behaviors or routines are most important in your daily life?
- ⊙ What actions would you like to implement to inspire others?

In summary, your mission statement should embody the character of your person: what are the foundations of your character, personality, and moral compass? What is it that makes you *who you are?* The aim is to develop an individual mission statement that defines the person you are and reflects everything you wish to be recognized for.

Live Your Mission.

After you've created your personal mission statement, you can utilize the statement to steer your lifestyle. This is where the legacy-building process starts. You can make a wonderful personal mission statement, but nobody will ever know who you are when you don't follow through with the mission each day.

One method to ensure you play an active part in shaping your lasting legacy is to take the time to compose your own personal eulogy. Morbid? It's not really. A eulogy is a speech that praises a person in high regard. We know of it typically from funerals, but it's really a term of endearment. Actually, it's a good idea to consider the future in your mind and plan your course in life. Instead of calling it a eulogy, let's call it a legacy letter.

In the process of writing your legacy letter, **consider the following points:**

- ⊙ **Who you really are.** Look beyond any social roles you could play, like siblings, fathers, employees or business owners, etc. Instead, think about the person you truly are. Who is at your heart?

- ⊙ **What are your goals?** We all are looking to achieve something in our lives. What are you hoping to accomplish before you go to sleep? What would you like to contribute to the world, your family, work, and so on? If you don't know your goals, it's difficult to achieve them.

- ⊙ **What's important day-to-day?** The old expression that people "can't see the forest for the trees" is meant for people who become so involved in the specifics of a problem that they forget about the bigger picture. This same idea can apply to your legacy. If you're only focused on the everyday responsibilities of living (the trees), you could forget about your larger goal (the forest). When this occurs, it's easy to lose track and wander through the forest in a haze, which leads to the loss of opportunities to create your purpose.

⊙ **What is your ideal life?** If time, money, education, or any other obstacles you might have considered were not an issue, what would your ideal lifestyle be like? What would you do with your time? Who would you choose to associate with? What are the causes you would be aligned with? Make sure you know what you want in your life because only then can you make efforts to achieve it.

Today is the day to start planning your mission, your legacy. However, don't rush through the process. You can and should have many iterations that evolve throughout your life as you live and learn. Finding a purposeful and creative goal takes thought and time. Be sure you are building your legacy on the right foundation.

CHAPTER 2

The Foundation of Estate and Legacy Planning

You don't have to be great to start, but you do have to start to be great.

— Les Brown

The Power in Legacy Planning

When we think about legacy it's not hard to think about one of the most powerful singers of all time, Aretha Franklin. Ms. Franklin left a powerful legacy in music that inspired many, however, she did not have a typed up Will. We will discuss Wills in more detail in chapter five. Ms. Franklin's Will was handwritten. In fact, she had a few of them and one of them was actually found in her couch. She joins a long list of famous people who have all failed to properly plan for life after they are gone. This made giving her benefits to survivors extremely challenging. The court had to determine if the written will actually expressed her wishes. It has been a long process in court as they could not fully rely on that document. Many people think having a handwritten letter, a thought, or the fact that they told someone of their plans before passing means they can easily transfer their assets. This is far from the truth!

As we grow older and recognize that our time here is limited, our goal should be to do everything that ensures those moments count. We all wish to leave something important and meaningful to our loved ones and for the generations to follow. Our aim is to think about our children's future while taking the necessary steps everyday so we can provide the best for it. We must make sure that they will be looked after when we're no longer around to care for them. This is how the legacy plan can play a role. A legacy plan in place implies that you have formulated an asset distribution plan for your beneficiaries but also leave something of value to those who surround you. It is essential for everyone to leave a lasting and meaningful legacy that is consistent with the ideals that every person aspires to uphold.

One of the things I am inspired by is when I hear how someone's legacy impacted another without money. The individual who had a rough upbringing or may not have had the easiest road in life. One thing that is consistently valuable to them is not money but the person who inspired them, believed in them, invested in them, spiritually and emotionally. It was the person who saw in them something that they couldn't see themselves. Most of the time we focus on the money and wealth aspect of this and not the impact or influence. Legacy is the mark that you make, how you want to be remembered. It's the impact on the lives of others.

Legacy Planning is often associated with estate planning, but even though both are related in several ways, there is one fundamental distinction between the two. Legacy Planning goes far beyond just a simple distribution of assets, estate, and properties. This method focuses on the values and the things that a person leaves behind, regardless of their financial circumstances. It's more about the feelings your heirs experience when they think of your life than they do about the financial or physical assets. This kind of legacy can affect the people you love dearly. Wealth does go beyond the value of assets listed in your bank balance. Wealth is the chance to get an education, start a business, purchase real estate, and have financial security that you can give to your loved ones or to those in need. This is the power in Legacy Planning.

Estate Planning 101

The process of creating a plan for your final estate in the event of your death is called Estate Planning. There is way more to Estate Planning than simply getting a Will done. However, no matter how large or small, everyone has an estate. This is not reserved just for wealthy people, nevertheless, when you are wealthy you may think more about your legacy and how to protect it. Really good planning is more impactful for families with modest assets. In the event there is a loss of a family member and its impact is huge financially, a properly planned estate plan can single-handedly change the course of your generations to follow. If you are just starting out, here are some of the things that your current estate includes:

1. Everything you own

2. Your home/real estate properties

3. Automobiles

4. Checking/savings/retirement/digital assets or any other savings accounts

5. Life insurance policies

6. Furniture or any personal property

We must get to a place where we are not afraid to look at what we have. Looking at what we have allows us to see what we need to work on to secure a better future for ourselves and family. No matter where you are, believe that what you have amassed through your life up to this point has value and should be valuable to the generations or charities after. No matter how large or small, everyone has something valuable that they cannot take with them when they die. Estate Planning allows us to make a plan in advance naming people or organizations we want to receive the things we own after we die. It helps to make sure all of your property and financial affairs will be in order so that those who you care for will be taken care of in the event that you are no longer with them. Simply put, an estate plan allows you to create a broader plan of action for your assets that you may apply during your life as well as after your death. It is composed of eight components which we will talk further about throughout the course of the book.

The question you want to ask yourself is:

How do I want my world to look when I'm gone?

Better yet, how do I want what I worked so hard for to be distributed after I die or become incapacitated?

The eight components of Estate Planning are:

1. Wills
2. Trusts
3. Power of Attorney
4. Health Care Proxy
5. Living Will
6. Businesses
7. Real Estate
8. Life Insurance

Estate Planning is for everyone, not just when we grow old and are retired. You can start Planning when you are eighteen. Often people put off planning because they don't think they own enough, or it will be too costly and confusing. They also feel that the option is there to either build wealth or just wait until they feel like it, but unfortunately, we cannot predict how long we will live. Too many people do not plan, and we know that when we fail to plan we can plan to fail. What's important is we start wherever we are with whatever we have. The majority of time many people are focused on accumulating wealth but spend very little time in protecting it. Properly transferring wealth is essential to making sure that your hard-earned wealth is protected. With the estimated amount of $41 trillion to be transferred over the coming years, the need for specialized budgeting for the people who leave wealth or any kind of assets behind and for those who will be receiving it, is just the same as ever. The earlier you can put the plan in place, the more effective it is.

Leave a Mark not a Mess

When we talk about Estate Planning, people think it's all about dying. When we think about dying, it's not something we may be comfortable planning for, let alone talk about. However, we should focus on living, living with peace of mind and living with the knowledge and understanding that in the event that you do leave you won't be leaving a mess—you will be leaving a mark. The mark is a positive way. Making sure you have a well-planned and thorough legacy plan will save you from unnecessary procedures like probate, the court-supervised procedure of confirming the will. A majority of legacy plans depend on trust, which can eliminate probate entirely.

It is advisable to establish an existing plan to:

1. ***Make Informed decisions***: We don't want to live our lives in ignorance, we want to make informed decisions on some of the things we can do to secure our future. It's important to get financially organized and know what your assets are so that none of them are lost.

2. ***Save family thousands:*** When you go through life and do not make a plan, typically it will cost your family money just to access your assets. It also can save you money if you grow older and need care. Especially if your insurance doesn't pay for it and you don't want to have to spend out of pocket. This is what planning for life can do for you.

3. ***Assets are not lost:*** Asset protection planning which we will cover in chapter three has become a major reason people are calling and meeting with me now. They want to ensure their assets are not lost and are protected in the event that a lawsuit comes up. Numerous people don't know that every state has a department of unclaimed funds. In the state of NY alone they have $13 billion in unclaimed assets. So many people pass away with assets that were not claimed or passed on to the next generation because no one knows about it. So it just sits there. We want to prevent that and anything that could happen while you are alive.

4. ***Protect family from outsiders and family:*** We know that not only is it that outsiders can prey on your assets, also family members. Family members can go at it when someone passes away. One of the things I always hear is that I can't believe my family is acting this way. Especially during these mourning times. This is one of the main reasons you should plan for life! You can prevent family drama and expensive legal costs by taking the time and designating a guardian and trustee for your minor children if they are underage, or beneficiaries who are of age. If the beneficiary is of age but potentially bad at

managing money, then you can create an estate plan that will protect them and make sure they don't squander their inheritance. It's extremely important to designate a trustee.

5. ***No Court No Drama:*** We avoid the family drama and avoid going to court when we plan right.

6. ***Be Prepared:*** For whatever life brings or comes up.

How to Make a Legacy Plan

I'm sure if given the choice to choose where your assets go you would want to make sure it was distributed correctly to the beneficiaries you choose. Handled by your family and not by the courts. The best time to plan for life after is now. I know it can be a challenge to think about our own deaths or the possibility of not being able to make decisions on our own. We don't want to be in a position where our family is caught off guard and not prepared when death or incapacity strikes us. What's important is to put something in place now that you can change later as things change in your life. When you are aware of the importance of having a Legacy Plan, it's fairly simple to begin this process. Start by creating the list of your Legacy Plan and then follow it through to collect the necessary information as well as documents from the past. **All you have to do is adhere to these guidelines:**

- ⊙ Find out your core values along with the legacy you would like to leave behind.
- ⊙ Make a list of the assets you have.
- ⊙ Decide how to divide the assets—who will be the inheritor of your wealth?

- Consider ways to make this world a more beautiful one. Have you thought about making a donation to a charity or helping others who are in need?

- Is there any particular preference regarding your medical care?

I like to say get into the habit of planning and making changes at every milestone in your life. Like getting married, having children, or moving. It's also advised to make changes when getting divorced, one of your beneficiaries passes away or there's a change in your financial circumstances. When you know that you have a plan in place, one that you control and has instructions on how to protect your family after death, you can give not only your loved ones a peace of mind, but you will have one as well. In addition to Legacy Planning, Estate Planning is one of the most considerate things we can do in our lives that can greatly impact the ones we truly love. Once you have the answers to the questions, you're only one step further closer to securing your plan for the future.

Key Takeaways:

1. Legacy is the mark that you make, how you want to be remembered. It's the impact on the lives of others.

2. Legacy Planning goes far beyond just a simple distribution of assets, estate, and properties.

3. Looking at what we have allows us to see what we need to work on to prepare to secure a better future for ourselves and family.

4. Estate Planning is for everyone, not just when we grow old and are retired and not just for the uber rich.

5. We should focus on living, living with peace of mind and living with the knowledge and understanding that in the event that you do leave you won't be leaving a mess—you will be leaving a mark.

6. Creating a plan allows you to:
   - Make informed decisions
   - Save family thousands
   - Avoid loss
   - Protect family
   - Avoid court and conflict
   - Be prepared

7. Get into the habit of planning and making changes at every milestone in your life.

CHAPTER 3

Protect Your Assets

"Someone is sitting in the shade today because someone planted a tree a long time ago"

— Warren Buffett

What is Asset Protection?

Have you ever made a mistake, or have you left any part of your business or life open to liability? What I mean is have you ever been in a position where you could be or have been sued, such as in claims or bad debt? How about bankruptcy?

Anyone who owns a business, real estate, or any other asset of value will want to ensure they legally protect themselves from risk or anyone who might wish to sue them. Asset Protection puts vehicles in place that preserve and transfer wealth to the next generation. Asset Protection can be viewed as a kind of insurance that covers all of your assets and ensures they are safe and secure. Typically, if we hear the words Asset Protection, many people think of it as these foreign concepts with all these hidden roads they have to take to get to it. Trust me, it's not as complex or intimidating as it sounds. Asset Protection is an idea of legal strategies to prevent creditors from accessing certain assets without violating the law. Which in turn ensures your wealth is maximized to serve as a launching pad for the next generation.

While people don't expect for these possible legal troubles to happen, and in most cases they don't, when and if they do, you want your assets to be protected. In other words, important assets can be secured. Like home or auto insurance, Asset Protection is there just in case something happens. In the case of death, we can be certain it will happen someday, so it is important to have a plan to address wealth transfer. It covers all of the work that you put into building your wealth, creating your legacy, as well as any assets of value.

There are five key areas of life situations where Asset Protection is major:

1. *Death*

So much wealth is lost in failing to protect assets prior to death. Some families are not aware of the wealth, so it's never claimed or received. This huge oversight causes assets to be left in the department of unclaimed funds, each state has one. Currently, the largest unclaimed asset is five million dollars in an investment account. Unfortunately, this wealth will be spent on legal and court fees due to poor planning. Wealth can also be stolen by predators preying on family members who are ill prepared to take care of the assets of another family member after death.

2. *Business Owners:*

Business owners are doing a lot of things day to day. In particular, entering into contracts and dealing with third parties. Because of this dynamic, a lot of liability can come up. This also leaves the window of claims and lawsuits wide open. In particular, employment law. If you have a business that employs people, employee claims are a huge area that could be an issue. Years ago, a person sued McDonald's after accidentally spilling hot coffee in their lap and suffering third degree burns. The person was later awarded one million dollars. Today, there is caution language on McDonald's coffee cups warning about the hot temperature.

3. *Professionals:*

Doctors, lawyers, CPAs, and anyone who has a professional license are vulnerable for lawsuits, debts, and liabilities.

4. *Real Estate Owners:*

Anyone who owns real estate, whether it's one property, multiple properties, or commercial (particularly if there are tenants), there is a lot of room for lawsuits and other issues. With tenants, there are people staying, or coming in and out. Anything can happen. A landlord once told me about a lawsuit she was in due to a child falling from the balcony of her rental property where his family was renting. This is likely a scenario one would not anticipate. These are the risks that property owners face.

5.   *High-Net-Worth Individuals*

Individuals with a significant amount of assets typically become a target for lawsuits. In today's world, with people having access to the lives and information of celebrities and entertainers, they are being sued for just about anything. Why? Because in some cases, just to make things go away, there may be a settlement, even if it's not true. People will look for any misstep to try to get paid. There was a story about a woman in California who was walking while conversing on her cell phone. She was not paying attention and walked into a construction site. She got hurt by a ladder. While there were signs and the area was closed off, she ended up suing and getting a six figure settlement. This is just one example of another person being careless, but the company and or individual had to pay for the accident.

Why You Should Have Asset Protection

One of my clients was recently in a car accident. He had a DUI against him but didn't seem concerned about the probability of a lawsuit happening. Shortly after, a lawsuit was filed against him by the person who was injured. While the person waited a few years, my client started to get concerned because he had assets and wanted to protect them by transferring them. Here was the problem. Once you have a lawsuit against you, and if it's been ongoing for a while, you cannot then transfer your assets to protect them. While there are ways and strategies to do so, transferring assets after a lawsuit is filed against you is not the best way to protect yourself financially because it can be construed as a fraudulent transfer. The reason it would be fraud is the person knew they were getting sued and knowing the assets would be attached, transferred them to protect them. Certainly not the time to do it. In every area of building a legacy and creating wealth, you must plan ahead. It's simple, before you do anything ask yourself: "Am I covered in case an issue arises?"

The creation of an Asset Protection strategy before the time of any lawsuit puts you in a strong position to avoid putting your assets at risk. It can stop the possibility of a lawsuit because it makes it impossible for anyone to place an attack on your assets. As the debtor, if you think there's a chance of an individual making a claim against you, it's time to act swiftly to secure a favorable outcome. With a little planning, you will be better placed to protect the wealth that you've put so much effort into building. There are legal options you can take to safeguard your assets from the threat of a lawsuit, claim, illness, or death. Planning for Asset Protection is beneficial for the debtor. It deters those who want to target them from bringing the appropriate lawsuit.

If someone succeeds in bringing a lawsuit against you, then chances are you're going to lose your property or a portion of it, based on the court's ruling or settlement. In order to avoid these instances, asset owners, through Asset Protection strategies, should add layers of liability protection and insurance. For instance, like the example above, if the landlord is sued and that property is in their name, then all of the assets in their name are vulnerable. If, however, the landlord owns the property in a limited liability company, then the vulnerability remains only with what is owned by that limited liability company. We'll talk more about this in later chapters.

Knowing the requirements of the state is essential when it comes to protecting assets. The primary function of Asset Protection is to help owners of assets protect them in a legal manner. It makes sure that when insulating assets, individuals and even businesses are not engaging in illegal actions like hiding assets, bankruptcy, or fraud.

Three Things to Consider with Asset Protection

If you implement Asset Protection in the correct manner, individuals are additionally able to gain the use of these strategies as mentioned above. The benefits for an individual could include preserving the wealth for their family members by holding assets that could aid in getting the loan from a bank.

Here are some aspects to consider when exploring various options for protection:

1. *Start planning early:*

It is best to start implementing security strategies for your assets as soon as you can. If you wait too long, you might not be able to protect your assets as you're trying to. If, for instance, you discover that you could face an action in court and you want to hide assets at the last minute, it is likely to result in more trouble than good. If you wait until you are sick in the hospital or facing a terminal condition, then it will likely not afford you the opportunity to implement the right plan to preserve your assets. If you're able to start early and implement the appropriate safeguards, you will not be blamed for using any strategies to avoid issues when legal concerns occur.

2. *Find out about the various types of strategies for asset protection:*

If you want to ensure that your resources are adequately secured for the long term, it would be beneficial if you invest your time researching various options and kinds of protection plans for assets offered on the market. Consult with an attorney to understand your options. Your plan should be specific to you, your family, goals, and circumstances. When you know the details of your options, you will be able to make the best informed choice.

3. *The goal is to balance the control vs security:*

When you are looking for the ideal plan to protect your assets, it is possible to select a plan that grants you the most amount of control with less protection. The more control and flexibility you have with your assets, likely the less degree of protection. Which is okay, you must do what makes sense for you. The contrary is that you can get the maximum amount of protection over your assets with the least amount of flexibility and control. The best place is usually a happy medium.

A lot of the strategies mentioned can seem confusing and complex, especially when initially starting out. It is not necessary to be in a panic. If it feels overwhelming, reach out to an attorney or trusted advisor who can help you put the correct plan in place to protect your assets.

Key Takeaways:

1. Asset Protection puts vehicles in place that preserve assets now and transfers wealth to the next generation.

2. Asset Protection is an idea of legal strategies to prevent creditors from accessing certain assets without violating the law.

3. The creation of an Asset Protection strategy before the time of any lawsuit puts you in a strong position to avoid putting your assets at risk.

4. If you're able to start early and implement the appropriate safeguards, you will not be blamed for using any strategies to avoid issues when legal concerns occur.

5. The goal is to find a happy balance between control and security. Don't panic. Keep calm and Plan!

CHAPTER 4

Preparing For The Unplanned

"Good preparation is better than hope for a miracle."

— Sunday Adelaja

I f you're not prepared, a single error can cause all of your hard work and success to be ruined within a matter of seconds. Understanding how to be ready for unexpected events is crucial to success in your life. We all know the phrase "preparing for a rainy day." While that may seem like an exaggeration, it is possible to make plans to be prepared for moments in your life in the event of an emergency.

Unexpected events can put undue stress on your financial stability and if unprepared can potentially leave you in disarray. Although you cannot predict the situations you'll face in your life, there are ways to be prepared for unexpected events. The loss of a job or an expensive car purchase can be handled much better when you have an insurance plan to draw on.

Three aspects to consider when planning for the unforeseeable:

1. *Emergency Fund.*

It's essential to save; however, it's difficult to figure out what amount should be allocated for unexpected expenses. Typically an emergency fund is composed of funds that can pay for three to six months' living costs. However, if you can put aside more than six months' worth, this way, you'll be able to cover financial obligations longer if something unexpected happens. If you do not have extra cash to create the fund completely, save what you can every month and then include the emergency fund in your budget. Remember that *you are richer than you think.* You would be surprised at how quickly you can save a good sum of money just by starting and being consistent. One of my friends, on a modest banking salary as a single parent, saved two years worth of living expenses, which came in handy when she unexpectedly lost her job and took two years to find a new career. A good goal is to aim to save 70% of your income and live off of 30%. It's a tall order, but however close you can get to that ratio, will make a big impact on your nest egg.

2. *Insurance.*

With a reliable insurance policy, a lot of the auto, medical, and home-related expenses can be covered partially or entirely. These policies are there to protect you and your wealth, so that if something unforeseen occurs, you are covered. Life insurance and disability insurance are also worthwhile to consider. Life insurance will take care of your responsibilities when you are gone, and disability insurance will replace your income if you are hurt. Although insurance will not cover all unexpected costs, it could be a huge help if you are in a financial bind. Consider the future and find out more about life, health, auto insurance, and homeowners insurance to protect your money and future.

3. *Budgeting.*

Incorporating emergency savings into your financial plan is the initial and most crucial step in making plans for the unexpected. However, there are additional aspects to budgeting, which is simply creating a monthly financial plan. Having a monthly financial plan could aid in financial security. Budgeting deals with creating a list of your expenses and financial obligations, subtracting those from what your income is for the month and making a plan for the rest. A key to budgeting that can help you stay committed is to include your savings, investments, and entertainment at the top before you get to bills. This is how you pay yourself first and reap the benefits of your labor while committing to your responsibilities. Knowing your overall budget can help you understand the distinction between needs and wants. You can also prioritize expenditures and, if required, make adjustments to accommodate the unexpected costs.

While we can't anticipate any unexpected situation, we can prepare for the most significant and likely ones by conducting our homework. You may not consider it important even when it's smooth and easy. However, you'll be more equipped to overcome the difficulties and be more likely to get over them when troubles arise.

Long Term Care & Disability

Every person should make financial decisions that are crucial for financial security and peace of mind, ranging from various kinds of insurance, to saving and investing money to planning for your future. One important but often ignored aspect of a financial plan is disability insurance. This helps to offset the financial burden of an injury or illness that prevents one from earning an income.

Your earnings are often the largest asset you have. If you take the amount you earn now and divide it by the length of time you anticipate working, then you'll be aware of how much financial protection could be diminished in the case of an illness or injury. The estimated length of an illness could cost a worker earning $50,000 per year, a cost that could grow to $3.8 million in the future. For those who are at higher income levels, a disability may be a major shift in their way of life. I know of a doctor that purchased disability insurance and got hurt on the job. He is now retired getting a substantial amount of money from his policy for the rest of his life because he thought ahead.

Even a short-term disability may be a serious financial burden as a long-term disability could be catastrophic. Your employer may offer a type of disability insurance; however, it will likely not be enough. Therefore, you might need to consider private coverage.

It's hard to know if you'll need to go into a nursing facility or require the aid of a home health worker, but one thing is certain: the cost of these services are astronomical. According to a recent study, the national average for a private room at a nursing home is $84,000 annually. I usually talk to clients who are approaching 65 about the opportunity to get long-term care insurance. It is possible that you do not need to invest in this type of insurance, but you should be aware of the cost you might be liable for if you suffer from an illness that is chronic or becomes disabled and unable to take care of yourself for a long period of time.

Long-term care insurance benefits are provided to those who, as a result of an accident, illness, or advanced age, require assistance with carrying out at least two everyday activities (such as bathing, eating, dressing or toileting, as well as transfer).

Have the "insurance conversation" with your family members to ensure that you and your family members are properly secured.

Health Care Proxy

Mr. and Mrs. Sandy were married for 60 years. They were a sweet couple who were madly in love, even in their late 80's. They were very close and happily spent all of their time together. Mrs. Sandy became ill and was undergoing treatment for cancer. It appeared that Mr. Sandy was well, but it turned out that Mr. Sandy suddenly became ill and ended up in the hospital. He needed surgery to improve his condition, but he refused the surgery. Mrs. Sandy. along with their children, believed he was not in his right mind. They wanted to make the decision that he should have the surgery. Unfortunately, they could not because he didn't have a healthcare proxy in place, and Mr. Sandy passed away shortly thereafter.

A health care proxy document is a legal instrument that allows a person to represent in making healthcare decisions for another individual. While many people only think of healthcare proxies when they're older, it is not necessary to be terminally ill or even old to establish a healthcare proxy. This can come into play if you become incapacitated and can no longer make rational health related decisions.

Everyone is able to and should have an existing healthcare proxy. It is never too early to have a plan in the event of a tragedy that will cause you to be incapacitated and require medical attention. The person you select to be your healthcare proxy can only make medical decisions on your behalf when it is determined by a medical professional that you are not in a position to express your wishes. Certain states require that you have a doctor who declares you disabled for the proxy to be able to take over the decision-making. Your healthcare representative could make life or death-related decisions for you, and the person you choose to trust must clearly understand your health desires and your faith-based beliefs.

The person you choose can make a variety of crucial medical choices on your behalf. They also perform the following tasks:

- Speak to your doctor
- Prevent or approve treatment or operations
- Decide whether to utilize artificial hydration or nutrition
- Make organ donation decisions
- Choose a healthcare facility of choice
- Review medical records for decision making

You can name anyone to act as your health proxy, such as an individual from your family, a friend, or trusted associate. You should designate a second and third person as alternate proxy in case the primary proxy is unable or unwilling to perform. This is not an easy thing for most people to do so you really need to be sure that you are selecting the person who will make sound, levelheaded decisions.

A comprehensive healthcare proxy will also discuss the potential circumstance that one will need a guardian or conservator to care for them if they cannot care for themselves. If an adult loses the ability to make decisions for themselves, care for their finances, or perform their daily self-care duties, they may be determined to need a *guardian* or a *conservator*.

> A *guardian* is a person or agency who will govern or control one's day to day care.

> A *conservator* will manage and control the financial and legal aspects of the person's life.

Everyone is empowered to make these decisions for themselves to save time, energy, and money. Even more importantly, you will choose the quality of life that you desire and deserve.

Health Care Proxy & Your Living Will

A healthcare proxy should be accompanied by a living will. A living will, not to be confused with a will, gives instructions to your healthcare proxy on what decisions to make if you were terminally ill. This includes, medical treatment, nutrition, life prolonging treatment, etc. Based on your state, a healthcare proxy may be combined with a living will in one advance directive document.

In a living will, your proxy must be informed of *these* details concerning you:

- ⊙ Your views on health as well as death and illness
- ⊙ The medical treatment you prefer, such as the life-sustaining treatment and comfort treatment
- ⊙ Religious beliefs
- ⊙ Concerns about caregivers, doctors, and hospitals

Here are four important questions to be answered in your living will :

1. What kind of care and treatment would you prefer if you were in a terminal condition?

2. What would you do? If you had suffered a brain injury or were in a coma and weren't likely to fully recover?

3. Do you wish to be placed on life support, such as a respirator or feeding tube?

4. What would you do if you could not do it on your own, without relying on others?

How to Get a Healthcare Proxy

It's a straightforward process to designate an individual to act as a healthcare proxy; however, every state has specific laws that govern the procedure. **The majority of states adhere to these steps:**

Step 1. Fill out the form for a health proxy with information such as your name, date of birth, and date that the contract is signed.

Step 2. Choose the person you want to designate for your medical proxy.

Step 3. Add any conditions or specific requests such as DNR or refusal of life-extending interventions. You may also restrict the authority of your proxy or grant specific powers.

Step 4. Sign your healthcare proxy and get it notarized. Certain states may additionally require the signatures of witnesses.

The person you choose to be your health proxy is an important decision. **You should keep these points in mind when choosing the person to fill this important job:**

- Who is able and willing to make informed decisions regarding your health?
- Who will represent you in the event of your becoming incapacitated?
- Be sure to let them know that they are listed as your health care proxy.

⊙ Give your proxy the complete information regarding your desires and requirements as you can.

Most people choose a close relative as your healthcare agent; however, you are able to choose any person to serve as your representative. Once you have informed the person you want to be your healthcare proxy, you must engage in a lengthy and detailed conversation about your medical needs.

Power of Attorney

I was speaking at an event some years ago and a woman in the crowd shared a story. She was a realtor representing a family. The family was in the process of selling their home for financial reasons. The home was in the father's name. The father fell ill and had a stroke. He was alive but unconscious. The family could not complete the sale without the father. They needed a power of attorney to be able to continue the sale on his behalf. The problem was that since he lost the capacity to understand his affairs and the consequences of his decisions, he could not give consent nor sign a power of attorney. So often people contact my firm in haste, that someone is ill and the family needs a power of attorney to plan for their assets, or access bank accounts to care for the person, or protect property, or access personal medical and financial records, and in many cases I have to break it to them that there is not much that we can do in that respect. You must put a power of attorney in place while you are well and in your right mind. If you wait until you need it, it may be too late.

A general power of attorney is a document that allows you to give authority to another to make legal and financial decisions for you in the event that you cannot. Many people think this is not a necessary thing because they don't realize the importance of having one ahead of time.

Creating a power of attorney allows you to give powers to control the following:

- ⊙ Real estate and personal properties
- ⊙ Motor vehicles
- ⊙ Tax matters
- ⊙ Stocks and bonds
- ⊙ Financial institutions
- ⊙ Insurance
- ⊙ Electronic communications and digital assets
- ⊙ Retirement plans and benefits
- ⊙ Deal with business interest
- ⊙ Family maintenance
- ⊙ Estate planning

These powers are broad and generally are unlimited unless you state so specifically. I usually explain to clients that as a measure, you must ensure that the person you select as your agent is one you would trust with your debit card.

Take a deep breath and understand that planning is for the benefit of your loved ones. Often we don't want people in our "business," even our loved ones. This is not the time to be selfish and/or stubborn. We must keep in mind that life does happen as we age. It's important we set the proper plans in place so that in the event that something does happen, our families are not left holding just an emotional loss but a financial one as well.

Key Takeaways:

1. Although you cannot predict the situations you'll face in your life, there are ways to be prepared for unexpected events.

2. A good goal is to aim to save 70% of your income and live off 30%. It's a tall order, but however close you can get to that ratio will make a big impact on your nest egg.

3. Consider the future and find out more about life, health, auto insurance, and homeowners insurance to protect your money and future.

4. A key to budgeting that can help you stay committed is to include your savings, investments, and entertainment at the top before you get to bills. This is how you pay yourself first and reap the benefits of your labor while committing to your responsibilities.

5. Get educated on the cost of long-term care and disability insurance, these circumstances can bankrupt your family in the long run.

6. Everyone is able to and should have an existing healthcare proxy.

7. You must put a power of attorney in place while you are well and in your right mind. If you wait until you need it, it may be too late.

CHAPTER 5

The Importance of a Will

"To know even one life has breathed easier because you have lived. This is to have succeeded."

— Ralph Waldo Emerson

Fifty-five percent of Americans die every year without a legacy or estate plan. An even staggering seventy percent of African Americans die every year without one as well. Here is what we must really think about, one hundred percent of us will die. There is no escaping that. While this is a very tough pill to swallow and a hard fact, it's true. Yet, we must come to terms that this will eventually happen. Knowing this, while it can be scary, planning for the moment that will one day happen should be our number one priority. Why is this important? Well, no one has a time clock on their lives, but I'm sure if they had a choice they would choose to see their next generation living lives of meaning because of what was created by them. Families should not have to worry about where money is coming from, where opportunities are coming from, or what to do financially after a member dies. While having these conversations at any time with family members or an attorney can seem very uncomfortable, what's even more uncomfortable would be leaving your family behind without proper care, struggling not just emotionally but financially as well. There is a remedy for these types of worries, and families can take action today. With a little simple planning you can make a tremendous impact on the direction of your legacy.

One of the most common pieces of your legacy plan is a Will. A Will is probably the first and most important document anyone thinks of when they are preparing to leave their assets. A Will is usually the beginning of the story, it's not the end, and for most people it's not going to be the only thing they need to secure their legacy. However, a Will is one of the most important foundational documents you should have when you are trying to protect your assets, properties, or are trying to create a legacy for your family. A Will is a legal document that sets forth your wishes regarding your desire to distribute your property and care for your minor children. There is no minimum amount of assets needed to create one. When you don't have, at minimum, a Will in place, you leave decisions about your estate in the hands of judges to determine what happens next. A Will can help to ensure that your assets go to the people or organizations that you choose. The key word here is YOU.

With a Will YOU CAN:

- ⊙ Be clear about who gets your assets and how much.

- ⊙ Determine who will manage your assets

- ⊙ Decide who should care for your minor children without any court involvement.

- ⊙ Direct where your assets go (to ensure they stay out of the hands of people you don't want to have them).

- ⊙ Provide funeral instructions.

- ⊙ Ensure your beneficiaries get access to your assets much faster.

- ⊙ Save money for your family.

When people pass away without a Will, these wishes may not be carried out. Not having a Will can cause loss of time, money, and emotional energy to settle any of your affairs after you are gone.

Often what people don't realize is that even when you have a Will it means:

1. Your loved ones will not automatically get an inheritance.

2. It will not keep your family out of court or out of conflict.

When one dies, their loved ones must submit their Will to the courts for a process called probate. Probate can be a very long and expensive court process for your loved ones. While you can prepare a Will for yourself to be completely sure everything is in order, it is recommended that you have your Will prepared by an attorney. In some cases, a Will is beneficial, in that it's certainly better than nothing. When it's well drafted and clear cut, you are telling the court exactly what to do with your assets. It's a better avenue than intestacy.

Dying intestate means that a person dies without a Will, and the courts will follow the plan the state puts in place for those who don't plan. When you die intestate (without having a Will), the laws of your state determine who will inherit your assets as a default. The laws differ from state to state, but generally, the distribution would be made to family members, including your children and spouse, grandchildren, parents, and then cousins, etc. The state's plans often reflect their idea of how people typically decide to distribute their estates. It also provides protections to certain beneficiaries, especially minor children. This plan could or might not be the best fit for your needs, and some of the built-in "protections" may not be required in a harmonious family.

Why You Should Have a Will

Whether you pass away with or without a Will, a lawsuit must be started against your estate for the benefit of your creditors first, then your family. This estate administration lawsuit takes place in the surrogate's court. If you die with a Will, then your estate goes through a similar lawsuit, through a process called Probate. What happens in these court proceedings? The court allocates the person's assets to their next of kin after a lengthy process of notifying all of the person's possible heirs and creditors. Your estate will be responsible to pay all the parties involved, including your lawyer, property appraisers, bond fees, executors, and the court fees of course. In some states it can be more costly than others. Typically these fees make up 5% of your estate. The court then makes sure the deceased person's debts are paid and the remaining assets are allocated to the correct surviving beneficiaries. Think about working hard all of your life only to pass away and have everything you've worked so hard for in the hands of a court or government.

Recently, two brothers James and John purchased a home. James wanted to buy a property that he could live in, but he unfortunately could not qualify for the home by himself. So he asked his younger brother John if he could help him by co-signing on the property. John agreed. He had no interest in the property at all–he wouldn't be paying for it. The only thing he did was help his brother James and become an owner of record. They purchased the property and all was well. Later on, John had a child and planned to get married. Unfortunately, John was killed in a tragic motorcycle accident. He did not have a Will or any other legacy plan in place; his half of the property is going to his daughter. We know the home is not John's property; he only wanted to help his brother James out, but he had no Will, no planning documents. The way they held the title to the property is a term called "tenants in common." Tenants in common means if a co-owner dies, the deceased person's interest passes to their heirs or the person specified in the deceased person's Will. We will talk more about how the title is held in chapter eight on real estate. Because of this, half of the property is going to the child, eventually, when the child is of age, and a surviving spouse if any. Now James' property is at risk and has diminished by 50%, and John didn't leave anything to give that back to his brother. He also did not leave a life insurance policy for his daughter and/or brother that would have potentially paid a significant portion of the home off.

A Will is a great addition to an estate, but as stated earlier, for most, it is not the only thing needed to ensure your wishes are respected. In this case, a trust would have provided the brothers the outcome they wanted in the most seamless way without court interference. We may think we are doing all the right things in the world, talking about what we want to accomplish and even planning, but these types of incidents happen ever so often over and over again. If John had a Will he could have stated who should receive his assets. In this particular case he could have said, "I want my interest in the property to go to my brother James," and that would have solved the problem. It should also state who is in charge of making sure their gifts get distributed to the right parties. Like money in the bank, stocks, art work, cars, etc. Who would make sure this happens? That's called an "executor," and that's someone whom you would name in your Will. Besides that, your Will should say what's going to happen to John's minor child. John could say whom he wants to be the guardian over his child's inheritance. A Will could also say if you want your assets to go to someone other than family. Whomever you choose. A Will is extremely valuable because in the event of a tragic accident, it's literally you directing where assets go after you are gone.

When planning with a trust, a Will is often still a companion to trust planning. The type of Will that accompanies a trust is called a "Pour-over Will. A "Pour-over Will" will serve as a safety net to ensure that if there are any assets that you owned in your name personally, your Will, will direct the court to transfer that to your trust and accordingly your trust will take over from there. This makes any court involvement streamlined and limited.

Choosing an Executor for Your Will

There is an important question you must ask yourself and that is: "Who can I trust to take care of my assets when I am gone?" After you pass away and your Will is accepted for probate, your Executor should be appointed by the court to step in and walk out your wishes. It is necessary to name a living individual to act as executor of the estate.

The executor should be:

- ⊙ Someone you trust and is responsible
- ⊙ Someone in good financial standing (if not, your Will needs special language)
- ⊙ Someone patient and emotionally grounded
- ⊙ Qualified individuals - i.e., parties over 18, U.S. Citizens

Usually an adult child, spouse, or a trusted relative or friend, is the person who manages your estate. You can also nominate executors who are joint, like your partner or spouse, as well as your attorney. The role of an executor is a big responsibility. This means that the person needs to be someone you trust with your life after death. So the size of your estate should not matter. The probate court typically supervises the executor to make sure they fulfill the provisions of the Will. If your situation is complicated, it may make sense to consult an attorney, someone who has financial and legal knowledge in preparing a comprehensive Will. If your situation is complex, it is likely that you need more than just a Will.

If your estate is significant (ranging in the millions), or your legal situation is complicated, it is best to hire an attorney. If this is the case, make certain to choose an attorney who is well-versed in the laws of your state and has a wealth of experience making Wills. The American Bar Association of your state may assist you in identifying a lawyer who is suitable for you. Make sure the language of your Will permits this and allows your executor the flexibility to deal with the relevant issues not explicitly stated in the Will.

Wills and Minor Children

A Will is absolutely necessary to confer guardianship of minor children. This is critical for single parents. We do not want your children to end up in the care of the state. For single parents, the odds are twice as high that your child could be left without a parent. Where I usually find the greatest concern is: the custodial parent does not want the other parent to have custody even if the custodial parent was deceased. I've had various clients who have had many valid reasons– the other parent lost custody due to their instability, or inability to provide, or not being in the child's life at all. I've even had a client who wanted to make sure the father and his family were excluded from raising the child, fearing for the child's safety and to prevent inappropriate relationships. These are all valid reasons. It's important, especially in these circumstances, that not only does the custodial parent have a Will, but that they document any evidence or reasons why the other parent should not have primary custody. Why? Because if the custodial parent passes away, the surviving parent will have stronger rights than anyone else recommended in a Will. The Will will serve as evidence, along with other supporting documents, as to why the court should follow the deceased parents wishes as to whom to exclude from the child's life. Without this, the court could very well unknowingly put the child or children in harm's way. In addition to stating long-term guardians in your Will, you should have short-term guardians detailed in legal documents. Why? Because as you can gather, anything that goes through the courts takes time and money. Having guardianship transferred to a designated person will not be instant. You do not want your kids in the hands of the state under any circumstances, when there are willing, able-bodied, fit adults of your choosing to step in. These documents will allow authorities to know and trust that the individuals you stated are fit to care for your children temporarily while the court process is figured out. This is especially important in unexpected accidents. Who can you select? Family members? Friends? Loved ones?

Why You Should Update Your Will

As discussed, your Will will probably be one of the most important documents you will ever draft. The challenge is after the Will is done most people never look at it again. However, you should update your Will every time you experience a major change in your life. Typically, you want to update your Will at minimum every three (3) years. Lives change everyday, so it's important to update your Will at every major milestone.

The following are some of these milestones:

- ⊙ Marriage
- ⊙ Birth of a child
- ⊙ Divorce
- ⊙ Move
- ⊙ Retirement
- ⊙ Downsize
- ⊙ Financial circumstances change significantly
- ⊙ Purchase or sell real estate
- ⊙ An executor or beneficiary listed has passed away

If there is a major change in your life, then it's important that you update your Will. It is always best to think of it like this: "If something should happen to me today has my Will been updated to reflect my current circumstances?" All families are unique. Especially yours. Don't allow the court to assume you would want your assets to go to your spouse, kids, parents, siblings, and so on if things change. But families have unique situations, some don't want to leave anything to their family, some have individuals who are like children to them, some have best friends and family friends that they want to bless, as well as nieces and favorite nephews. So if YOU don't update your Will, YOU will not have the legacy you desire.

Key Takeaways:

1. No one has a time clock on their lives, but I'm sure if they had a choice they would choose to see their next generation living lives of meaning because of what was created by them.

2. Although a Will is not the end of the story, for most people to secure their legacy it is one of the most important foundational documents one should have when trying to protect your assets, properties, or creating a legacy for your family.

3. A Will can help to ensure that your assets go to the people or organizations that YOU choose.

4. When you die with only a Will, a lawsuit must be started against your estate for the benefit of your creditors first, then your family in surrogate's court.

5. A Will is absolutely necessary to confer guardianship of minor children.

6. You should update your Will every time you experience a major change in your life.

CHAPTER 6

How to Protect your Legacy with a Trust

A myth about a Trust is, it costs too much to have one done. However, dying without a Trust most often will be more expensive than dying with one.

— Sabine K. Franco

What is a Trust?

A Trust is a legal document prepared by a party for the benefit of the beneficiary(s). It is a vehicle that allows the creator to get their wealth to the next generation without court interference. In this document, the creator of the Trust, commonly known as the Trustor, provides instructions to a Trustee concerning the ownership and power to control their assets. The instructions determine how someone's assets should be handled and distributed when the person is alive and after their death. A Trust allows legal protection and preservation of the Trustor's assets should the Trust creator die. Trusts can be structured in various ways. You can design exactly when and how assets will pass to beneficiaries and dictate the terms of inheritance quickly without court interference. The Trust should contain a schedule which details all of the assets that belong to the creator. This schedule informs the family of the extent of the estate without any guesswork.

Families who have at least $100K in assets and or real estate will likely be good candidates for a Trust. Assets must be transferred to the Trust in order for the Trust to exercise its control over the Trust's assets and carry out the instructions of the Trust. A Trust has no power if it is not funded.

When you die, the Trust makes transferring your assets easy. It helps maintain privacy, which avoids predators who are looking for financial gain against your loved ones. It also helps to preserve your assets by eliminating court costs and **avoiding time delays,** which happen when you pass without a trust.

When people envision planning, they want their loved ones to have it easy, and seamlessly take over their assets without a problem. Having a Trust affords you the opportunity to help achieve this goal. When creating a Trust you will want to appoint a beneficiary. Anyone can be a beneficiary. You get to decide. Family, friends, companies, charities, anyone living or in existence at the time of the creator's death. The creator can even give instructions for the Trust to create an entity, or charity, or an account to direct Trust assets after the creator's death.

Five Reasons to Create and Establish a Trust

There are many different types of Trusts today. The type of Trust you choose will depend on your assets and your goals. Trusts are not for everyone. Not everyone has the right circumstances or amount of assets necessary to start a Trust or may not really need it. This is why legacy planning is personal to your needs. It's very specific to you. There are five reasons you may want to get a Trust:

1. ***To avoid Probate Court***: A Trust allows your family to benefit by avoiding all of the hurdles imposed by the probate court or more accurately described, surrogate's court. In most states, surrogate's court costs families about 5% of the estate, give or take. These costs include attorneys fees, court fees, valuation fees, bond fees, etc. If one has assets in multiple states and dies without a Trust or with only a Will, then the cost can be more.

2. ***Saves time:*** Establishing a Trust reduces the delay in getting your loved ones the benefit of your assets. In many states, probate or administration can take upwards of six months to a few years should the estate become contested, or if case-specific issues should arise.

3. ***Establishes control***: With a Trust you have much more control over your children's experience after your death. You can dictate who will manage the funds of your child or appoint an individual to be their guardian. Some individuals instead decide to leave their assets to a family member to care

for their children after death. I caution against this because once you leave an individual a death benefit, you are giving them free will to do as they wish. Without a Trust or Will, your family member would have no obligation to abide by your wishes. In the alternative, funds within the established Trust can be used for health and educational expenses, maintenance and support of your children and anything else you desire. **Your wealth is in your control.** You can specify the terms of the Trust in detail, determining how and when distributions can be made and for what specific purpose. For example, a Trust can ensure the welfare of beneficiaries who suffer from a mental or physical impairment that could hinder their ability to manage their care and finances.

4. *Waste:* You can also prevent waste with a Trust. With a Trust you can set milestones (ages, or stages of life) for your loved ones to benefit from your Estate, whether partially or in full. The Trustee can distribute assets in increments according to your wishes. For example, if you have a million dollar life insurance policy, you can determine payments to be made to your minor beneficiary as follows: Once the child finishes high school, $10K is distributed, after college completion, $20K and so on.

5. *Avoid family conflict:* Trusts create a definitive plan with certainty and peace of mind for your intended beneficiaries. This helps to limit conflicts with family as the plans of your

affairs remain private, only being disclosed to those who need to know.

The Two Types of Trusts: Revocable vs Irrevocable

Although there are many types of Trusts, any Trust option would fall under the umbrella of either a Revocable or Irrevocable Trust.

1. *Revocable Trusts*

My client's wife recently passed away. She had a Revocable Trust. The challenge here was she was married previously, and the ex-husband was the Trustee under the Trust. She failed to update it upon remarrying. Under the Revocable Trust, she had the option to change it at any time prior to her death. After her death, the Trust became Irrevocable, and her assets were controlled by her ex-husband rather than her new mate under the provisions of the established Trust.

The term "Revocable Trust" refers to a Trust that can be revoked, changed, or amended in whole or in part, also often called a Living Trust. This Trust can be altered or canceled in any way, at any point, as long as the grantor remains alive, is deemed competent, or legally provides an individual the power to make decisions on their behalf. In a Revocable Trust, you have full access to your assets presently and can add to them, remove them, change beneficiaries, etc.

While a Revocable Trust protects your assets in the sense of ease of transfer upon death, they do not offer protection from lawsuits, creditors, or claims during your life. This is called liability protection. A Revocable Trust can be coupled with business entities to provide a level of liability protection where appropriate. Upon the death of the creator, a Revocable Trust becomes irrevocable, meaning it cannot be changed. This locks in the creator's wishes for the protection and benefit of the beneficiaries.

2.   *Irrevocable Trusts*

Princess Diana left a trust for Prince Harry. She experienced what it was like to live under the strong arm of the monarch. As we've learned in recent news, it can be a depressing place to be with no way out. Presumably, Princess Diana didn't want this for her kids. When she divorced she gained $30 million dollars plus $1 million a year in annual salary. She created a Trust for her children. Each of her sons were given $11 million, which turned into $18 million over the years due to compound interest of the investments made within the Trust. So as we learned, when Harry and his wife could not deal with the oppression and control they experienced on the throne, he decided to renounce his role and position and therefore wealth. However, he was coming into the age where he would have access to the Trust created for him by his mother to fall back on. Her sons received dividends at age 25 and the rest of the funds at age 30. Imagine how proud and honored she would be to know that she was there for her son years later when he needed her most. In their most vulnerable low moment, she's there even after her death. Harry also received an inheritance from his grandfather, and presumably will receive one from his grandmother, the Queen of England.

This Trust was likely an Irrevocable Trust, meaning unchangeable after her death, with distributions left at specific age milestones or life stages. This means once a person dies their Trust cannot be changed, so the wishes they put in place are permanent.

One can also create an Irrevocable Trust during their lifetime. These Trusts are often more complex, however, they are usually created to preserve assets, making them worth the investment. An Irrevocable Trust can't be modified. Irrevocable Trusts have strict rules based on the goals of the creator. Irrevocable Trusts are often used because they provide tax savings. Unlike Revocable Trusts, Irrevocable Trusts can be used for liability protection against lawsuits, bankruptcy, creditors, medicaid, government, etc. Especially for those in particular professions that are prone to being sued, such as lawyers or doctors.

Creating an Irrevocable Trust and adding assets to it serves as a way to remove assets from your ownership and estate. Assets transferred to the Revocable Trust still take on the identity of the creator for tax and legal purposes. While the Irrevocable Trust is completely separate and apart from the creator. It is like gifting those assets away to another entity. As such, the creator has much less control over those assets. Irrevocable Trusts provide more protection and less control.

Dynasty Trust

Protecting your children or loved ones with an Asset Protection Trust for life is also known as a Dynasty Trust. In a Dynasty Trust, your children will have the luxury of benefiting from the income of the Trust assets but never actually own the Trust assets outright in their name. After the death of a beneficiary, the next generation receives the benefit. Once the Trust is established, the Trustee must continue to invest its assets for long-term growth, allowing future generations to benefit from it, even those not yet born. As the creator, like other Trusts, you can set up rules on who can benefit from it, and under what circumstances. You can protect the Trust from the beneficiaries' creditors or divorcing spouses. A beneficiary cannot give up, sell, waste, or renounce his or her claim in the Dynasty Trust either voluntarily or under pressure. This makes Dynasty Trusts a great source of income for your family for generations.

There are five key benefits of a Dynasty Trust:

1. **It is almost 100% protected from creditors, divorces, claims, bankruptcies, or wastefulness.** The beneficiary never owns the assets personally. The assets are owned by the Trust.

2. **Assets can still be invested in real estate, stocks, and businesses.** If assets need to be pulled out of the Trust by the beneficiary, they can do so at the discretion of the Trustee, according to the rules and directions in the Trust. Otherwise,

beneficiaries will generally benefit from the income from the trust as directed by the creator.

3. **Beneficiary Control.** The Dynasty Trust can allow responsible beneficiaries to have complete control and access to their Trust assets. For beneficiaries that are not as financially responsible, the Trust's language may limit their access to Trust income or principal. However, for maximum protection, limiting the beneficiaries' access or allowing the beneficiaries to limit their access will prevent creditors of a beneficiary from attacking Trust assets for debt, or prevent the divorcing spouse of a beneficiary from trying to get to Trust assets.

4. **The assets can be held and protected for a lifetime.** Dynasty Trusts are long-term Trusts created specifically for descendants of the creator. They are truly Multi-generational Trusts. Dynasty Trusts can survive 21 years beyond the death of the last beneficiary alive when the Trust was written. If you were setting one up today, and you had a two-year-old grandchild, your Dynasty Trust could last well over 100 years. Long after you're gone, a Dynasty Trust can distribute income and principal exactly the way you would have wanted. Certain states have no limit on how long these Trusts can last.

5. **Beneficiaries can be co-Trustees with the selected Trustee.** Beneficiaries have an opportunity to become a co-Trustee, learn the ropes, and be part of the management of

the Trust, understanding the wealth and how to preserve it, while maintaining the ability to resign if needed to protect the Trust assets.

The Role of a Trustee

The Trustee is in charge of overseeing the assets under the Trust and distributing them as instructed under the agreement. Similar to selecting a beneficiary under a will, the creator of a trust has the freedom to choose anyone as a beneficiary. Beneficiaries who are at least over eighteen may also become Trustees. The Trustee is usually a trusted family, friend, accountant, lawyer etc. If you don't have a Trusted person or persons, you can place a Trust company in charge of your Trust. This is common with large complex Trusts. Note that the Trustee can also utilize professionals to facilitate managing the Trust's assets and maximizing the value of the assets.

The **Trustee will have the power** to borrow, loan, invest, take care of beneficiaries, receive and purchase life insurance, run or start businesses, deal with finances and accounts, etc. A Trustee can conduct business, own and manage assets, invest, purchase, sell, etc.

A Trust allows the creator to select a successor Trustee to immediately step in, in case the Trustee becomes incapacitated or dies. This makes for ease of transferring any assets to the Trust upon the Trustee's incapacity.

Key Takeaways:

1. A Trust is a legal document prepared by a party for the benefit of the beneficiary(s).

2. Families who have at least $100K in assets and/or real estate will likely be good candidates to have a Trust.

3. Five reasons to get a trust–to avoid probate, save time, establish control, waste, and avoid family conflict.

4. The term "Revocable Trust" refers to a Trust that can be revoked, changed, or amended in whole or in part, also often called a Living Trust.

5. Unlike Revocable Trusts, "Irrevocable Trusts" can be used for liability protection against lawsuits, bankruptcy, creditors, Medicaid, government, etc.

6. Dynasty Trusts are a great source of income for your family for generations.

CHAPTER 7

Use Your Life Insurance to Create a Legacy

"People need life insurance not only because they are going to die but because they are going to live."

— Dr. Marius Barnard

I n a recent study, 46% of Americans did not own a Life Insurance policy, however, what we do know is that 100% of us will all die someday. We have insurance policies on our cars, homes, phones, and even health in the event of a loss or sickness, but a Life Insurance policy is something people fear. The main reason people fear talking about Life Insurance is: it's another tough discussion about what happens when you die. Instead, the focal point of the conversation should be that not only are loved ones covered should you die, but having a Life Insurance policy can create an immediate financial legacy.

So what is Life Insurance? Life Insurance is a contract between a person and an insurance company that in exchange for your premium payments the company pays a lump sum known as a death benefit to whomever you decide will receive the benefit after you die.

So why aren't 100% of people insured if they know they will all one day die? It's simple, they either fully do not understand the importance of it, or the financial impact they can create for their family members in the future. When we decide not to be insured, or feel it's not needed at the moment, we put our family members at risk. Meaning, the risk of not creating an instant legacy, a loss of income and future financial opportunities for a spouse and children.

Some reasons why people feel they don't need Life Insurance are:

- ⊙ They don't understand what it does and why it's important
- ⊙ They feel that since they do not have children, it's not necessary
- ⊙ They may think they are too young as it is only for older people
- ⊙ It makes them think about death too much
- ⊙ The Life Insurance provided by their employer is enough
- ⊙ It's not a top priority
- ⊙ I'm healthy
- ⊙ It costs too much

All of the above are myths. The younger you are, the more affordable life insurance is. Properly understanding what Life Insurance is and can do can be a major tool to provide a family's income and cover expenses upon death. It can also be a tool to create an impactful financial legacy by creating a stream of income for generations to follow, allowing your beneficiaries the opportunity and advantages to benefit from having a large sum of cash paid out in the event of one's death.

In today's world, many families are barely surviving financially. One unexpected death, especially from a main income provider, can be detrimental to the family's lifestyle. If you have ever experienced the death of a loved one or heard of someone dying without a Life Insurance policy, then you know the turmoil it caused the family, not just on an emotional level but a financial level as well. The family is left to scramble over funds to cover a burial and any other outstanding debts. Think for a moment about the impact you can truly have by simply having a Life Insurance policy in place, knowing the payout of it can change the direction of your family's financial legacy. Life Insurance should not be thought of as merely associated with death, but as a way to enrich your life and the lives you leave behind. If you don't have $250,000 or $1 million lying around that someone can access immediately upon your death, Life Insurance is a sure way to add immediate liquid cash to your legacy. Even if you do, Life Insurance can also serve as a tax shelter and a savings account that can provide for you during your life, especially during retirement.

Funding a Trust with Life Insurance

Recently, a client's husband passed away. He had a Life Insurance policy and named her and their son as the beneficiaries. Upon the husband's death, the wife received her portion of the policy. However, since the son was a minor and the father did not have a trust, his son had to go to court to receive his share. There was a problem here–the court did not deem the wife credit worthy. This meant they did not trust her with the minor's funds and instead appointed another party to oversee the funds meant for the son. This posed an issue as it reduces the death benefit as the party overseeing the funds now has to be paid to do so. Had the father created a trust and made the trust the beneficiary of the Life Insurance policy, the trust would have given specific instructions as to what to do with the policy and would not have needed the court to determine who controlled the funds.

In chapter six we talked about the power of a trust, its benefits, and the various ways to fund it. Now let's talk about how a Life Insurance policy can be allocated for such a purpose. If you create a trust as we discussed, you must fund your trust with an asset. In this case, your asset will be a Life Insurance policy, **which will do the following:**

- ⊙ Keep the trust active
- ⊙ Ensure that your trust can control what happens to those assets

We fund our trusts by:

- ⊙ Making the trust the beneficiary of your assets

Or

- ⊙ Having the title or ownership in the name of the trust–meaning, the trust owns the asset

A Life Insurance policy can be a great way to fund your trust. If you pass away, the Life Insurance policy would pay out to the trust. The trustee would be able to manage the trust's assets and use the funds provided by the Life Insurance to care for the children, pay off a home, offset taxes, or just provide liquidity for any necessities. The trust can and should require that the Life Insurance funds be invested, to continue to grow and benefit from compound interest while owned by the trust. The trust and Life Insurance are a way to provide for minor children, because younger families do not typically have enough money or other assets to cover the impact of losing the head of their household. Life Insurance can give you peace of mind that the person(s) you leave in charge of caring for your children will be able to do so without any undue burden on them.

There are many types of Life Insurance policies. Listed below are two distinctions to understand:

- ⊙ *A Term Life Insurance policy:* A Term Life Insurance policy only protects you for a limited number of years (the term) and does not build cash value. This is the most inexpensive and cost-effective way to pass on wealth to your beneficiaries and create a significant financial legacy. In the event of an unexpected death, a term policy pays a death benefit if you die within the term. The drawback is that if you outlive the term, the policy expires and you get nothing. You may not be able to get a new policy due to age or health. Having adequate coverage for your lifetime is important while healthy.

⊙ ***Whole Life Insurance policy:*** Although more costly, a whole life policy provides more benefits to the insured during their life. Such as the ability to build cash value, borrow against the cash value tax free, borrow for any reason without a credit check. You can provide for business needs, investment needs, long-term care needs. Should you need to borrow against it, the full amount continues to grow and appreciate in value. In addition, the cash value is protected from claims and lawsuits, etc.

It is important to consult with a qualified Life Insurance professional and your attorney to find out which policy is best for your financial needs and overall financial plan.

Four reasons to consider funding a trust with Life Insurance:

1. **Funding a Trust with Life Insurance provides capital quickly**. Often your assets consist of things that cannot be used to meet financial needs unless sold. However, it may not be the right time to sell property or a business, etc. Trying to sell real estate or pull equity out in a short amount of time may be a significant challenge. Life Insurance can provide a solution to this predicament.

2. **Covering burial costs and end of life expenses**. Most people don't have enough cash in their bank accounts to cover the cost of a burial and legal costs to close out their or their family member's estate.

3. **Preserving other assets for greater gain**. Stocks, 401k, mutual funds or any other investment accounts may have significant tax implications if funds are withdrawn. You can preserve these assets, allowing them to continue to grow until the appropriate time.

4. **Instant legacy**. If your estate did not have a significant amount of assets, you can provide an instant surge of cash to leave the type of impact you wish to have on your family.

As you can see, having a Life Insurance policy is a quick, tax-free way to build wealth and fund your trust. While you don't need a trust to have a life insurance policy, a trust can ensure those funds are used in the way you decide. While there are many other ways you can fund a trust, life insurance should not be overlooked. It is the most straightforward and can be the most cost-effective way to create immediate wealth.

Create a Family Bank with Whole Life Policies

Many people may have never heard of the term "Family Bank." A family bank or infinite banking is a family funded entity that offers financing only within the family. Its purpose is to pool the family's resources together so that all participating family members can benefit. In short, family banking is a smart and effective way for estate planning. It is for anyone who wishes to build wealth, improve cash flow, and have financial independence from banks and lending institutions. It starts by older family members providing funds to the family bank which finances the next generation members' interests, business ventures, education, and any other options. In short, it allows for the next generation to get a head start in life. The strategy is to keep wealth in the family and keep it growing from generation to generation. This is done by using permanent high cash value Life Insurance policies to build a multi-generational bank. This bank grows and safeguards actual dollars while providing opportunities for family members to participate in growing and/or borrowing against the policies. There are various ways you can benefit from creating a family bank.

- **Grows assets:** Using a permanent Life Insurance policy such as a whole life policy in your family bank creates a safe and reliable financial growth strategy. Simply put, it is a safe and guaranteed option for funding your bank.

- **Supports entrepreneurship:** A Family Bank, which can be a trust and/or a business entity, can be used to support entrepreneurship. Your family can borrow from the bank to invest in or start business ventures. Or, the family bank can invest in a family member's business venture under the terms set forth in the governing document.

- **Allows financial flexibility:** A Family Bank allows the flexibility and freedom of the family members to pursue what they desire, without the constructs of society and its standards, but rather according to the family's collective goals and desires.

- **Family members can borrow:** Families can use the Family Bank to help them through college, a down payment for a home, or to start a business.

- **Teaches financial skills:** Creating a Family Bank helps your younger generation learn to talk about money and the value of it long term. It also helps them prepare to write a business plan and how to apply for loans and obtain loans if need be in the traditional sense.

⊙ ***Estate planning benefits:*** Having a whole Life Insurance policy in place allows the Family Bank to facilitate generational wealth transfer. Here you can allow insurance policies to be held, grow, and passed on tax free. This maximizes what's available for the family to benefit from.

⊙ ***Leaves a Legacy:*** Having a Family Bank is much more than a financial strategy, asset, or method for passing assets through your generations. It's an opportunity to pass along strong family values, priorities, habits, stories and more.

While it's important to have a Life Insurance Policy, it's even more important the way in which you use the policy. Knowing the impact you will have on the generations to follow, you will no longer associate dying with Life Insurance. With the right strategy, you can use your Life Insurance to create wealth and leave a lasting Legacy.

Key Takeaways:

1. Having a Life Insurance policy can create an immediate financial legacy.

   Properly understanding what Life Insurance is and can do can be a major tool to provide a family's income and cover expenses upon death.

2. You may fund your trust with assets such as life insurance, which both keeps the trust active and ensures that your trust can control what happens to those assets.

3. If you pass away, the Life Insurance policy would pay out to the trust. The trustee would be able to manage the trust's assets and use the funds provided by the Life Insurance to care for the children, pay off a home, offset taxes, or just provide liquidity for any necessities.

4. Life Insurance can give you peace of mind that the person(s) you leave in charge of caring for your children will be able to do so without any undue burden on themselves.

5. A Term Life Insurance policy only protects you for a limited number of years (the term) and does not build cash value.

6. Whole Life Insurance provides the ability to build cash value, borrow against the cash value tax free, and borrow for any reason without a credit check.

7. While you don't need a trust to have a Life Insurance policy, a trust can ensure those funds are used in the way you decide.

CHAPTER 8

The Way to Protect Your Real Estate

It's important that you understand the way in which you hold your Real Estate title. The right way will ensure it's protected and properly transferred after you pass.

— Sabine K. Franco

Real Estate Deeds

A young man once called me for assistance. He explained that his mother passed away unexpectedly. She owned property that was intended to be for him. As he further explained, his mother left the property in the name of his uncle. Though not the intent of the mother, the uncle requested that the young man pay him to transfer the property. The young man could not qualify for a mortgage because he did not have adequate income nor sufficient credit rating. Unfortunately, there is nothing that we could do to force the uncle to transfer the property that is legally vested in his name.

His mother just didn't know the proper way to provide for her son. It's unfortunate and happens quite often in varying scenarios.

People don't usually think of deeds as an Estate Planning mechanism, however, it is one basic way to plan how your property will be passed on after your death. It is a legal document that you can use to plan what will happen with your property once you are gone. It ensures it goes to the right party. How you hold title is a simple way to make sure that your property gets to your loved ones according to your plan.

Each piece of real estate within the United States is tracked or recorded, and the recording is made public. The ownership of property is memorialized by the owner's name being on the deed/title to the property and being recorded in the land records of the county or local municipality where that property is located. It is important that once an individual or entity's name is placed on a deed, that ownership is granted to that person. I begin here because many are unaware that this very action dictates the gain or loss of real estate from one's possession, ownership, and legacy.

A deed is a legal document that reveals the name and determines the owner of a particular property. It confirms the transfer of ownership from the previous homeowner to the new owner of the property.

When you purchase a house, you sign a deed as well as receive title insurance for the property purchased. This is accomplished by conducting a title search of the history of ownership of the property to verify that no liens exist against the property and to ensure that all of the property rights have been transferred along the way. How title is held on a deed can affect how that property is passed down to a loved one whether or not you have an estate plan. You can mistakenly disinherit a loved one of your real estate if it is not titled as intended.

Most homeowners don't know that there are numerous ways to hold title and their degree of protection varies.

You Can Hold Real Estate Title in a Few Different Ways

You can hold title in a few different ways. The way in which you hold title varies and depends on your circumstances. Before purchasing any property or if you already have, consult with an attorney to ensure you are properly holding title. This guarantees that you are protecting your property and passing it correctly. There are a few ways you can hold title, they are:

1. **Tenants in Common.** This is the way that two or more persons (co-tenants) can acquire or hold ownership of property, intending to have their interests in this property separated from each other upon the death of one. In the event of the death of one of the co-tenants, their ownership interest in the property is transferred to their inheritors according to the terms of their estate plan or by way of the laws of intestacy if they fail to plan. The surviving co-tenant continues to own their interest in the property as co-tenants with the inheritor of the deceased co-tenant. For the inheritors to acquire legal ownership, they must submit an application to surrogate court. Unless in fact, a trust was established for the portion of property belonging to the deceased co-tenant. Some states

provide tenants in common ownership as a default form of title ownership by two or more individuals where the deed is silent as to how title is vested. If the parties want to ensure title is held as tenants in common, the deed should state "as tenants in common."

2. **Joint Tenants with Rights of Survivorship**. This is the way two or more persons acquire ownership of property, intending to have their interests transferred solely to the survivor after the death of one. Contrary to tenants in common this happens automatically. There is no need for probate or administration. Also, if a trust was created but you have a joint tenancy stated on a deed and the trust did not own the property, the trust can be passed over. If this is not the intention, one that has joint tenancy on a deed should make that change. If a trust is included, the trust should have ownership of that asset via being listed on the deed. However, if the parties want to ensure title is held as joint tenants with rights of survivorship, the deed should state: "joint tenants with rights of survivorship."

3. **Tenancy by the Entirety or Community Property**. When married couples own property together, purchased during marriage, it's usually considered to be property of the marriage. This means if one spouse dies during the marriage, the entire estate passes to the surviving spouse without regard to any intentions. Similar to joint tenancy. If that is not the intention of the parties, they should state so specifically in

their deed. If the parties want to ensure title is held as tenancy by the entirety, the deed should state: "as husband and wife" or "as tenants by the entirety."

4. **Life Estate**. This specification on a deed reserves the right of a person to live on the property for their life before all the rights are transferred to those listed on the deed as receiving ownership. We call them remaindermen.

When transferring rights in a deed over time, there are a set of main rights that are passed with ownership.

Some rights include:

- Right to possess
- Right to control
- Right to use and enjoy without interference
- Right to allow others a right to use (licenses and leases)
- Right to privacy and to exclude others
- Right to disposition to transfer the property to someone else by selling, gifting, or inheritance
- Right to use property as collateral through a mortgage

When a life estate is created in a deed, the right to use and enjoy without interference is reserved for the person given the life estate. This way, property can be transferred without creating a tax burden or transferring capital gains. This is usually done when one wants to transfer their rights to real estate but wants to remain living in the property for life. Generally, an older or elderly person who is not seeking to sell, mortgage, or transfer the property otherwise and would simply want to remain living on the property. The life estate serves as a way to secure their interest while transferring all of the other rights to the remaining persons. When the life tenant passes away, the property vests completely in the remaining persons without any need for further action. It's automatic.

There are some things to be wary of

Merely adding a loved one to your deed causes them to take the position as an owner. Therefore, any appreciation (increase) in value that you would potentially pay tax on, if the property were sold, also applies to the person you added to the deed. This must be weighed against transferring property upon death, which would generally pass tax free. Note that once you completely transfer title to your property to someone, whether partially or completely, you cannot reverse it and you cannot force them to give the property back.

Deed to protect your real estate assets

As with the story of my client, one way for the mother to transfer property to her son is to add him to the deed. In the alternative, she could have also completed a deed transfer to her son reserving a life estate for herself. This would have preserved the tax benefit at her death and reserved her right to live in the property. However, since mom passed unexpectedly, maybe a life estate did not seem like the best option since she would not be able to refinance and have the flexibility of her ownership. She also could have kept the property in her name and drafted a Will leaving the property to her son. However, this would have taken time and money to get the property transferred to him by the court. If he did not have the resources, this could have proven difficult.

Leaving Real Estate in Trust

Another option which would give the young man flexibility and ease of instant transfer upon his mother's unexpected death would have been a Revocable Living Trust. Under this Trust, the mother could have transferred the property to the Trust and made her son a beneficiary

Real estate is the most common asset of families with wealth and often one of the most significant assets people have. As such, it is wise to use a Trust to transfer property as it contains an added benefit of protecting the beneficiary if the beneficiary is not in the ideal position to take title at the time of the gift.

Here are five things to consider with transferring real estate by way of Trust

1. **Revocable or Irrevocable:** With a Revocable Trust you maintain full control and ownership for life. You can make changes and you can continue to take advantage of the equity in the property by way of refinancing or obtaining a line of credit. Irrevocable trusts are less flexible. You can't change or dissolve the trust once you sign it and it cannot be reversed.

2. **The cost of transfer.** In order for your trust to exercise its control over your real estate assets, making it easy for your family to inherit, legal title must be transferred to the trust. In order to leave real estate in trust you have the upfront costs of creating a trust and transferring that real estate to your trust.

3. **Gifting to multiple beneficiaries**. When gifting assets through a trust it's easy to split real estate among multiple beneficiaries. This protects each beneficiary's interest in the real estate from not being vulnerable to potential claims, debts, or divorces of the others.

4. **Avoiding Probate in multiple states**. Gifting property in a trust when you own property in multiple states avoids probate in every state where you own real estate. This allows your loved ones to avoid probate in multiple states and preserves more of the estate assets.

5. **Using other assets to pay off the mortgage**. Gifting real estate through a trust allows you to ensure your loved ones can continue to maintain the property by providing other assets to pay off the mortgage(s), such as life insurance.

While you can create wealth through Real Estate, it is important to know that how you hold your title to your property will determine if you pass it properly to the generations that follow.

Key Takeaways:

1. Deeds are one basic way to plan how your property will be transferred after you pass and ensure it goes to the right party.

2. A deed is a legal document that reveals the name and determines the owner of a particular property.

3. Tenants in Common is the way that two or more persons (co-tenants) hold ownership of property, intending to have their interests in this property separated from each other upon the death of one.

4. Joint Tenants with Rights of Survivorship is the way two or more persons acquire ownership of property, intending to have their interests be transferred solely to the survivor after the death of one.

5. Tenancy by the entirety or Community property is a way to hold title by married couples which functions the same as joint tenancy.

6. Adding a loved one to your deed during life waives the tax-free transfer on death. You must determine which is more important.

7. It is wise to use a Trust to transfer property as it contains an added benefit of protecting the beneficiary.

CHAPTER 9

Legacy Planning Using an LLC

"With investing you are taking on responsibility. The more responsibility you have, the more things you must put in place to protect it."

— Sabine K. Franco

One of the best ways to protect your assets is by choosing an entity structure. Some structures offer no real protection for the creator, such as sole proprietorship or partnerships. While others, such as Limited Liability Companies (LLC) and Corporations offer a legal separation from the creator and the business. These are called entities. Business entities are separate from the creator, and they are formed to conduct business activities. They have a completely different identity and tax ID, which means it is not utilizing the creator's social security number nor credit. It's sort of like creating an alter ego as in Superman and Clark Kent. However, they must be treated as a separate entity, meaning apart from you. As a starting point, you want to consider which entity works best for you through legal protection, paperwork requirements, and tax options. As a new business owner you have the option to choose the way you set up your structure based on your needs. It's important to discuss with your CPA or attorney which works best for you.

The most common business structures are:

> *General Partnership*: a business arrangement by two or more individuals that share in all assets, profits and legal liabilities.

> *Sole Proprietorship*: a business that can be owned and controlled by an individual.

> *C-corporation*: C-corp owners/shareholders have limited liability and are taxed personally in addition to the corporation.

> *Limited Liability Company (LLC):* a business structure that protects owners from personal responsibility for its debts or liabilities and each other. Each member of the LLC reports the business profits and losses on their own personal tax returns instead of the LLC itself being taxed as a business entity.

In many cases, the popular choice for business structure is an LLC. An LLC is a legal business entity which is recognized in all 50 states. Many U.S. businesses are set up as an LLC due to the ease of running it and low documentation required to create them. An LLC is a way of structuring a business that protects owners from being personally liable for most of the businesses' debts and claims. It limits each member's liability as it relates to their business investments. In the event of a lawsuit, an LLC provides protection so the owner won't be found liable for debts and financial obligations of the LLC—their own personal assets are not at risk because it is sheltered by the business. You work hard to earn and build your wealth. You want to ensure your hard work is properly protected for the duration of your life, and it will be seamlessly passed on to the generations that follow.

LLCs, Trusts, and Wills Work Together

In chapters five and six, we talked about Wills and Trusts. We know that a Trust is a document, but the law makes it a container that you can actually put things into. Trusts and Wills can hold and own your LLC and other assets. Remember we talked about the flexibility provided by Revocable Trusts and the reality that the Revocable Trust does not exactly protect your assets from debts, claims, nor lawsuits. The prime feature of the LLC, however, is to provide liability protection, which prevents debts, claims, and lawsuits from extending beyond the assets in the LLC and vice versa. Coupling a revocable trust with one or more LLCs can provide you with the best of both worlds as a business owner and investor. You are able to shield most if not all of your assets in the LLCs, so long as they are being run legitimately and with proper record keeping. Having the LLCs owned by your revocable trust provides you with the flexibility to build and invest your wealth while having your plan in place.

The beauty of protecting your assets is that if something should happen to you there will be someone who can step in and manage the affairs of the trust—manage your businesses, upkeep your properties, care for you if you are incapacitated, or care for your loved ones. Much wealth is lost because people planned to fail, they put nothing in place, and due to a temporary illness or disability, everything is lost or damaged. Imagine being ill for a few months or having a surgery, etc., and not being able to deal with your affairs. One missed payment could derail your credit and throw all your plans off track. What if it was six months to a year? Having your businesses structured within a trust can help you keep everything on track. Your successor Trustee can step in and keep everything going.

How to Start Your LLC

While it's very easy and extremely tempting to start your LLC online, I highly recommend that you speak to a CPA or Attorney to properly navigate through the process. If done incorrectly, it can be deemed invalid.

To create an LLC you will need to:

1. Choose a Name

2. Get a tax ID number

3. Have an address that can receive official mail

4. File your articles of organization

5. Obtain business permits

6. Publish an LLC formation notice (only in a limited number of states)

7. Create an Operating Agreement

8. Pay the necessary taxes to keep your LLC active

9. Open a business account and apply for a business credit card

While this can seem like a lot to set up, it's important that you do not allow it to stop you from moving forward. These are vital steps for your business. Creating an LLC allows you to start protecting it. When looking to build your assets, or if you are thinking about protecting your current assets, you want to make sure the assets you have are not only protected but also have advantages by being protected.

Keeping the Proper Formalities When Operating an LLC

Recently, an individual started a payday loan company. These companies loan money to individuals and allow them to pay it back in installments. The owner created entities in states where these loans were restricted or illegal. He created a series of business entities, each owned by the other merely to separate himself from the entity that was doing the illegal activity. Since so many people were wronged, the government caught wind of the unethical practice and started to investigate. They found that these companies were not following any formalities. They were not adequately capitalized, kept no records, conducted no business; they were merely a front, purely created to try to shield and evade the repercussions of the owner's actions. The government would pierce the corporate veil of each company to get to him. The FTC sued him and won $1.6 billion and seized all of his assets. While this example is a complete case of fraud, this also proves that liability protection is not a blanket for shady dealings. You also must make sure your business dealings are in order. If you don't run the LLC like a business, even though your entity exists, it will seem as if it is only there for a front, or you are hiding things. In this case, the business owner was clearly trying to hide through LLCs.

One thing that people mistakenly do with their LLC is merge funds from their personal life and their business into the same accounts, and their expenses from both will all come out through the same accounts. This is called "comingling of funds." If you happen to be faced with a lawsuit or claim and they investigate your accounts and discover that everything is being paid out of one account, they can then use that against you as evidence, along with whether you're keeping adequate records. Do you have an operating agreement, and are you following it? Are you holding yourself separate from the company? If you are not adhering to the rules of running an LLC, essentially the government will ignore your liability protection and come after your personal assets as well. You should be able to show that the expenses from the business only come out of the business account. Note that a few mis-steps here and there won't be critical, but you certainly don't want to make a habit of it. The idea is to hold yourself as being separate from the business so the public knows they are dealing with a business that has liability protection. The key here is to maximize your liability protection by avoiding situations that will cause your business to be pierced by the authorities just to get to you.

The Importance of Having Multiple LLCs

For things that have liability exposure attached to it, such as real estate or a business where people can get hurt and injured, it's important to protect them separately, or protect you from their liability. We call these "hot assets" because they can put you in fire. Recently, a young lady who owned a few multifamily properties explained that unfortunately, one of her tenants who lived on the top floor, had a child fall from the balcony. While the event was unfortunate, the positive side for the owner was she did have her asset protected in an LLC, and she was not at fault for the child's falling. Had she been at fault and her investment property was not in an LLC, the tenant could have sued her personally and put her assets at risk. Additionally, the tenant could have gotten access to all of her assets in the lawsuit because her property was not in an LLC, or she had multiple properties in one.

Frequently Asked Questions (FAQs) on LLCs

If I already have an LLC that I'm running a business out of and I want to start another business, can I just use the LLC I already have?

The answer is I highly would not suggest it. As I mentioned earlier, if one of these assets is a "hot asset," then everything in that business is vulnerable. You cannot have all of your streams of income tied to each other; if one goes down, all can potentially be affected. If you have all of your streams of income tied to each other when you have a loss, you can lose everything. Having multiple entities helps to stop the bleeding. Again, your entities must be legitimate businesses being properly run to support the protection LLCs will provide.

Is it necessary to have more than one business entity?

While having multiple LLCs is perfectly legal and normal and there are no limits to the number of LLCs a person can register, it is totally up to the individual. Some investors may feel that instead of having multiple entities, they'd rather have a huge insurance policy that covers all of their investments, and they'd rather assume the risk of a lawsuit or some other issue that may arise. It depends on your risk tolerance. As an attorney, I'm of the mindset of layering on protection. The more protection the merrier. Also, insurance companies are always looking for ways they can deny claims. That's how they stay in business. The reason you want to keep your assets in separate LLCs is: if one of your businesses has a legal issue and that business owns multiple assets and streams of income (including properties), and that legal issue (depending on how severe), can impact everything owned in that LLC. For properties in particular, if there is a town issue or municipal issue, they can attach it to all of the other properties that are under that LLC umbrella. If all these assets were held in separate businesses, then liability is only to the extent of what is held in that business. Keep your assets separate. It's the best and smartest way to protect your assets.

What does having a separate LLC for each property/business allow me to do?

Limit the risk of any liability

When you create a different LLC for each property or business you own it limits any liability between the entities. For example, if you have multiple businesses or properties and one fails, the others are not at risk. Whereas if all are under the same LLC, each would be at risk. Real estate owners will usually form a new LLC for each property to ensure that in the event of a lawsuit only one property is affected.

LLCs are easier to divide

When you operate several businesses under one LLC, it becomes difficult to keep them separate and organize the paperwork and the assets. Having multiple LLCs makes it a lot easier to wrap up all of the loose ends and sell the whole business/property without worrying about confusion.

Having more than one provides distinction

LLCs are attractive for owning real estate and being able to collaborate in the event you want to invest with multiple parties or bring on investors for a particular business or project.

While becoming an investor may be extremely exciting, it should be equally exciting to think about what your overall protection plan will be going forward and how you can effectively protect your assets. LLCs are great for real estate for flexibility. LLCs can be a useful legal shelter in which you can pass down assets to your loved ones, minimizing or potentially avoiding estate taxes.

Key Takeaways:

1. As a starting point, consider which entity works best for you through legal protection, paperwork requirements, and tax options.

2. An LLC is a way of structuring a business that protects owners from the liability of most businesses debts and claims and allows each member's liability to be limited to what they invest in the business.

3. Coupling a revocable trust with one or more LLCs can provide you with the best of both worlds as a business owner and investor.

4. The idea is you want to hold yourself out as being separate and apart from the business so that the public knows they are dealing with a business that has liability protection.

5. You cannot have all of your streams of income tied to each other, because if one goes down, all can potentially be affected.

CHAPTER 10

Trademarks, Copyrights and Your Legacy

"Having your brand Trademarked is proven, not having one-you have to prove what you say is yours."

— Sabine K. Franco

P eople often ask if they should Trademark and Copyright their business and work. Specifically, if they should trademark their name and or brand and if they really need it. There are tons of reasons why you need a trademark as well as why you should copyright your work. Both protect creations of the mind. These types of intellectual property (IP) are assets that can be passed on as part of your estate and may be worth significant amounts of money. They can generate residual income for decades and in the case of Trademarks, forever impacting multiple generations. One of the biggest distinctions between the two is what they actually define. Trademarks are things like names or slogans, designs, and other items that identify an organization or product. Copyrights generally protect the contents of a creation. There are other forms of intellectual property such as patents, trade secrets, and trade dress, which we won't cover specifically.

Trademarks

In speaking with a client, she mentioned working over ten years in building her company and her brand. She had built her brand with tons of sweat equity. One day she noticed that someone else registered her trademark doing the same thing she was doing in a different place. The person was doing essentially the same thing, however, it was for a shorter time. The difference is the person with the shorter time trademarked the company. While this can seem like such a messed up situation to be in for the person who worked so hard for so long. This is why it's important to protect your legacy. When you are not trademarked and you want to sue the person you feel has taken your name, you are not guaranteed to win. You can potentially lose what you've worked so hard for, and it can be extremely costly. This can put you in a very difficult position.

> *Having a trademark is proven, not having one-you have to prove what you say is yours.*

Your trademark is the number one way consumers will find you, and trademarks are everywhere. Everything you see in public is trademarked. The things you see in the supermarket, clothing stores, billboards, etc., are trademarked. It's a guaranteed way to influence consumers. It's very important to get your trademark.

There are five reasons why you should trademark your brand:

1. ***It's easy for consumers to find you***: This allows consumers to know your company, and what type of products or services your company provides to the public. It allows consumers to pinpoint you and easily find you. It also distinguishes you from other companies. If you are a printing company and there is another printing company and neither of you have a brand that stands out to distinguish one from the other, it will be confusing to the public. A Trademark identifies the difference between the companies. If you are using a trademark, you may use the 'TM' symbol to indicate creative rights in the trademark. If you decide to register it, you'll earn the right to utilize the ® symbol. If you do decide to register your trademark, you must keep in mind that it could take approximately 18 months to be processed.

2. ***Brand Awareness***: A trademark is basically an exclusive brand name for a company—what makes it stand apart from other trademarks. The significance of registering a trademark is that a valid registration will prevent any other company from copying or making use of any portion of it to gain for commercial purposes. Brand awareness allows people to be aware of your brand. It can represent the lifestyle and or the mission of your company. Companies like Nike for instance have a brand when people see the swoosh, they identify it with quality. Their trademark speaks to that quality. It gives

you consistency over time so if you are operating under the same name, brand, or logo. People will start to see what you produce, and it will start to build a good will. People will depend on it; they can trust it, and this is how you build your company's personality through your trademark.

3. ***Trademarks can last forever.*** Trademarks can pretty much last forever. Once you get your trademark, you have five (5) years between your fifth (5th) and sixth (6th) year to file an extension to say you are still using it, this is how, and I'm providing all this proof that I'm using it the way I said I am. Once you have that, you are good for another five years. Between year nine (9) and ten (10) you have to do the same thing. Every ten (10) years after that you can file for another ten (10) years. There are tons of brands that have been registered for years. If you continue to extend your trademark, it can potentially last forever. It then becomes a true asset because it builds value overtime. When it builds value over time it's something that starts to appreciate. It gives you a competitive advantage. Why? The longer you've been around the more valuable the trademark is, and now the people who come in the market who want to compete in your space are competing against a company that has built a reputation, has equity, and people have a relationship with you. It also allows you to be leverageable. This means you can put up your trademark to get loans or to expand your business. You can use it as security just like a house is used as security for a

mortgage, your trademark is as well. It also can be used as passive income. If you want to license your trademark, lend it to someone else so that they can use it but they pay you to use it if you license it as passive income. Kellogg's, for example, started with cereal, now they have breakfast bars and cereal bars, much more than what they started with through licensing.

4. ***Trademarks are cheap***: Pepsi has been trademarked since 1896, think about how much their brand is worth at this moment and how many people all across the world know who they are. The initial cost of a trademark is literally pennies compared to the value your brand will be worth over time.

5. ***Trademark is like real property***: Trademarks can be bought and sold, assigned for use, put up for collateral license for someone else to use, or you can use it for character merchandising. An example of this would be Disney. Disney has bags, pajamas, dishes, crayons, everything that you can imagine, if there is a Disney character for them.

Your trademark registration grants you the sole right to use your mark to identify the products or services it covers. Using an ® symbol behind your logo warns other companies against using your trademark. It also permits you to bring legal action against anyone who has used your name without your permission. A registered trademark is yours, and you may allow others to use it through licensing it.

Copyrights

Copyrights are the rights a creator has in an expression which can include movies, audio recordings, sound, photos, broadcasts, artworks, literature, stories, literature, computer programs, sculptures and more. Those rights conferred to a copyright owner are to copy, adapt, distribute, perform in public, transmit digitally, display, and promote. These rights generally last for the life of the creator plus 70 years. The purpose of these rights are to give incentive to creatives to create the stated forms of work for the benefit of the public, culture, society, to enrich our experience in life. The incentive of ownership encourages this creativity. The requirements for a creation to be copyrightable is very broad because works of art are subjective. Copyright does not extend to words and short phrases, fonts, coloring, names, slogans, listings of ingredients or contents, symbols or designs. These will more likely fall into the category of trademark. Copyright also does not extend to a mere idea (meaning it has to be in a form that it can be perceived), plain facts, clichés, federal government work, procedures, processes, systems, methods, concepts, or discoveries.

The parameters are that it must be:

1. Original and

2. Have a minimal level of creativity.

Due to the vague broad description of the requirements, it's easier to understand what copyright is not.

Reasons to Copyright Your Works

I recently read a story about a photographer who took a photo of a sports professional in the act of accomplishing a monumental moment. The player, without consent, and probably thinking it wouldn't be a problem to use a picture of himself, used the picture on his social media page. The photographer sued the sports professional for using the photo because the picture was copyrighted. He won the lawsuit. In today's world of easy access via online, social media, and other forms of digital outlets, it's very easy to have work stolen and or duplicated without your consent. Although the sports professional could have justified the fact that it was him in the picture so it should be okay, the fact is the person who took the picture was the creator. To prevent your creative work from being stolen or duplicated without your consent, it's extremely important to have your creative work copyrighted.

The reasons to copyright your work:

1. You may prevent others from using your copyrighted work.

2. You can sue others who use your work without permission more easily.

3. There is proof of your ownership rights to be able to leverage them through licensing, sale, or transfer, especially in light of the rise of Non-Fungible Tokens (NFTs) as a valuable asset.

4. The benefit of licensing and leveraging your ownership.

As you can see, Trademarks and Copyrights are extremely important in protecting your legacy. The purpose is to protect your work and the creativity of your mind. It's important to trademark and or copyright what you're doing. It covers what you've worked so hard for, for yourself and your future generations. Understand that these are assets that you not only can leverage through ownership while living but can pass down to your loved ones for them to leverage as well. This can be through licensing to provide continued royalties and income.

Building your brand is important, but properly protecting it will determine the impact on your legacy.

Key Takeaways:

1. Trademarks are things like names or slogans, designs, and other items that identify an organization or product. Copyrights generally protect the contents of a creation. Both protect creations of the mind.

2. Your trademark is the number one-way consumers will find you.

3. Copyrights are the rights a creator has in an expression which can include movies, audio recordings, sound, photos, broadcasts, artworks, literature, stories, corporate literature, computer programs, sculptures, and many more.

4. This is not just to prevent the revenue loss from the company but also to safeguard its reputation, image, and its overall worth.

5. Understand that these are assets that you not only can leverage through ownership while living but can pass down to your loved ones for them to leverage as well.

CHAPTER 11

Now is the Time to Create Your Legacy

"There is no passion to be found playing small and settling for a life less than the one you are capable of living."

— Nelson Mandela

A Lasting Legacy

After the passing of Nelson Mandela, it is not difficult to appreciate the legacy he left behind. He was a man of integrity, a man for the people who believed in the absolute liberation of the human being from oppression. Because of this belief he was imprisoned for more than 27 years. Upon his release, he didn't want to retaliate against those who had taken away nearly one-third part of his existence. He was an authentic leader in every sense of the word. Nelson Mandela was always humble; he stood up for justice, taught us to forgive, and demonstrated that people are exceptionally resilient in difficult times. With the strength of mind to not just endure his traumatic experience, he also won the day against those oppressors who tried unsuccessfully to silence him as well as the millions of people he represented.

We all have that Mandela drive within us, one that, regardless of our adversity, we can be a part of the solution for generations to follow in our own unique way. We can develop strength within us and perseverance when times get difficult, and we feel we are unable to take on more. When we know what our legacy is, that gives us meaning in life. That meaning allows us to overcome the temporary setbacks and struggles that may seem difficult in the moment.

The legacy left by Mandela is that every life is worth living, and freedom should be the fundamental right of every man together with their loved ones. Freedom of movement, the ability to learn, as well as the freedom to work, live, and leave a legacy. No one should ever give up on their goal no matter how long it takes to reach. Even if it is twenty-seven years.

Now is the Time to Create Your Legacy

While you are here it's important for YOU to decide how life goes for you and your family regardless of your current circumstances. It's now time to create your legacy starting with having the hard conversations with your family. These difficult conversations are not meant to shed light on anything negative, but rather to see where you are so that you can make the proper decisions moving forward. Now is the time to plan to leave a mark and not a mess, a legacy and not a mystery for those we love the most.

You must know that you are empowered to impact lives, you are empowered to be a blessing, and you have the ability to create a powerful legacy for your future.

Some people live their entire lives not doing anything they love. Not giving all they have every single day. Every morning they get up regretting past decisions, mistakes, and what they are dealing with now because of it. With this negative mindset, there is no way proper planning for the future can be done. Leaving a legacy is not even thought of. We are barely getting through the days.

What we fail to realize is, when we don't see life as meaningful, valuable, and a tool to impact, we don't plan well. We live life in fear, and in most cases we don't plan at all. Worst of all, those that we intended to bless, the ones we say we care for deeply may not be the ones to benefit from our life if we don't intentionally and legally put a written plan in place and live up to our life's mission.

The process of creating wealth can feel like a puzzle in many ways. How is it that some people seem to be able to become wealthy while others are struggling to figure out how to get back on their feet or never seem to make it? It is because wealth is actually a mental state. You must make up your mind that there is a larger purpose in your life and commit to the purpose. Because you've made it this far, I know you are serious about your legacy. When you think of the word "legacy," what is the first thought that comes to your mind? Today, I want you to ask yourself the following:

1. What is my legacy?
2. What does the word legacy mean to me?
3. What do I want it to be?

4. What is something I want to spend my entire life doing and be remembered by it when I am gone?

5. What am I doing every single day that would leave an impact on the world daily?

6. What do I want to leave behind to my children and organizations?

7. Whatever I do leave behind, am I making sure there is something in place so that their world is better because of me?

8. Why not be the person to impact the way people look at adversity?

9. Why not be the person to wake up everyday and live the life of your dreams?

10. Why not be the person to motivate others?

11. Why not be the person to change the history of your family?

You Can Fulfill Your Purpose

So many people leave this earth with unfilled dreams, goals, and ideas. They tiptoe through life praying they make it to death safe and because of that, they don't have the courage to find meaning in life and live their greatest life. I want to tell you today, that regardless of what you may think or feel, *You are richer than you think!* It doesn't matter where you come from, what you've gone through, or even where you are now. What does matter is the riches that are within you and how the world will be a better place because you decided to tap in, show up today, and move forward.

What type of things can you say that would encourage people to change their lives for the better?

People are waiting to hear a voice, something powerful that resonates within. Perhaps you overcame something momentous that can and will inspire others. Why not you? This is your uniqueness and why you are here. The first step in creating your legacy is seeing the bigger picture so you can fulfill your purpose!

The Journey

It is important to understand that on this journey in life we all will be met with some sort of challenges that may cause us to question why? In fact, Winston Churchill once said, "Success is not final; failure is not fatal: it's the courage to continue that counts." In other words, the challenges we meet prods us to look for the courage within to keep going and striving toward our legacy. If you have not started your journey regarding your financial legacy, you can still be wealthy if you're willing to understand the key to creating wealth. How you consider wealth moving forward will determine if you are wealthy. It all starts with your thoughts. The solution to the problem of poverty is abundance; therefore, focus on the blessings present in your life today and build on that.

I can't stress enough how truly important it is to find our mission in life. That will directly impact your legacy. I can tell you, your mission is not to get up every day fighting a struggle or being upset with life because of circumstances. I can also tell you that you can't blame failure or mishaps on other people's inability to define what meaning is in their lives. Everyday, people find a reason to be fulfilled in life. There's a value they place on their existence; they know why they go through the challenges of life—so they can grow and become better people—because that directly impacts those around them. They make better decisions, they know setbacks are temporary, and they keep a positive attitude about life. I want you to truly think about what you may be dealing with currently and ask yourself, is what I'm dealing with more important than my future? Is it more important than making sure I leave an impact? Is it more important than me knowing that I overcame all of the heartbreaks, setbacks, and struggles because I was motivated to leave a legacy for not just my children but my children's children?

Time to Live Life SMART

How would you like the world to look and what would you like your children to remember you by? I define this as having **SMART** goals.

- ⊙ **Specific:** Being specific means you are clear on exactly what you want to accomplish, what you will use to get there, and having alternatives in case things don't pan out as expected. You want to be definite in your decision making. Note that your legacy plan is something that can and should evolve with you, however, making definite decisions allows you to be covered sooner than later.

- ⊙ **Measurable:** How will you know when you have accomplished the level of wealth and information necessary to walk out your goals and desires for your future generations?

Creating a plan with actionable steps allows you to create measurable milestones to accomplish those goals.

⊙ *Attainable:* Are your legacy goals achievable during your lifetime, or is there something you can put in place to make it achievable once you are gone? Is it feasible, and how will we get there?

⊙ *Realistic:* Are your legacy goals true to you? Are they true to your life's mission? Are they true to your purpose? If you were unable to accomplish these goals, would you see it as a missed opportunity?

⊙ *Timely:* Time is tricky. We don't know how much time we have. In legacy planning, we use our best estimate based on average age to put certain protections in place. But one thing is for sure: you should always have your basic plan in place sooner than later. Timely means as soon as possible and with a definitive date. Your legacy plan is something you can build on. You can start with the basics and build on it as you evolve, and your life bends and curves as most of our lives do.

Every day you wake up is a day you can begin to create your legacy. Your future is in your hands. No matter where you are today and what you think you may not have, always remember, *You're Richer Than You Think!*

Key Takeaways:

1. Regardless of our adversity, we can be a part of the solution for generations to follow in our own unique way.

2. You have what it takes inside to do all that you desire to do; every life is worth living to the fullest.

3. You are empowered to determine how and whom you will impact.

4. Even the smallest pebble can have a ripple effect that spans an ocean, you can be that pebble in your family.

5. There is no NEED to fear. It's not at all required. Live boldly and freely.

6. You are richer than you think!

7. Create **S**pecific, **M**easurable, **A**ttainable, **R**ealistic, and **T**imely (SMART) goals for your life and legacy.

Made in the USA
Columbia, SC
26 July 2022

64000701R00076